＃ The Feedstore Chronicles

Disclaimer

Bullshit.

Generally speaking, bullshit is thought of as a negative. As in…

I'm sick of his bullshit.
Don't bullshit me.
Or … That's bullshit and we all know it.

However, in my native state of Texas, bullshit and all bovine fecal matter, has a much better reputation. Here in the beef capital of the world the actual aroma is most often described as the smell of money. Bullshit's redeeming qualities extend beyond the feedlot. A natural and organic fertilizer, bullshit is a garden staple and, just as it does for plants, a heavy sprinkling of bullshit helps any good tale grow and flourish.

This book is no exception. While it is a fact I spent much of my youth working at a Texas feed store for an unabashedly nefarious boss, this book is a fictionalized account of those days, meant strictly as entertainment for its readers. No character in this book is to be inferred as an accurate or actual representation of any person, living or dead, as the traits, habits, and mannerisms of many were combined and meshed with my own imagination to create the characters contained in these pages. Other than my own, and the two pro wrestlers who had character enough to stand on their own, most names have been changed.

So what I'm saying is … take these stories with a grain of salt, maybe even with a squeeze of lime and shot of tequila, because bullshit tastes much better that way.

Chapter One

Every Dog Has His Day

Most coming-of-age stories are fraught with symbolism, hidden metaphors, and a heaping mound of other literary devices. Not this one. Not mine. You see, I came of age while working at a dusty Texas feed store. A place where *To Kill a Mockingbird* involved a twelve-year-old and a BB gun. *Of Mice and Men* was a problem easily solved with rat poison. And *David Copperfield*, nothing more than a dude who made shit disappear.

The spring of 1989 bloomed with me a rosy-cheeked boy of sixteen. Doyle Suggs was a twice-divorced, thirty-year-old high school dropout and mystical guru, of sorts, for the feed store crowd. On the surface, we held little in common.

Doyle ran a feed store in Amarillo, Texas. A joint called Pearl's Feed and Seed named after Doyle's mother. Originally she ran the place, but by the time I hired on, Pearl had long since hightailed it back to her ancestral home in Oklahoma.

Nearly all of Doyle's family hailed from the same rural Oklahoma town. A town famous for hosting one of the world's largest rattlesnake roundups. You have to wonder about an entire town that considers it high entertainment to track down and capture vast quantities of poisonous snakes. I don't know how the practice got started, but let's hope a group of teenage boys first hit upon that idea, since it's a proven fact pubescent males are the least intelligent demographic of humans. A demographic I solidly belonged to when I hired on at the feed store.

Even with the ignorance of youth working against us, neither I, nor any of my high school buddies, made a habit of seeking out venomous snakes. My friends were content to while away their time with the three *F's*—*Football, Fighting, and Fornication*. All washed down with six-packs of tepid beer since, as teenagers, we rarely could afford both beer and ice.

That brings us to me. Despite the fact I towered over most my age, I was too lazy to be any good at football, too accommodating to get in many fights, and too scared of my female classmates to find a willing partner for the latter of the F's.

But then, in the spring of '89, I went to work at Pearl's.

Like all sixteen-year-old boys, my desire for cold, hard cash was rooted in a swelling appreciation of the opposite sex. Foolishly, I believed a steady paycheck, and all the imagined things I could buy with my minimum wage windfall, would separate me from the pack. In my warped fantasy land, I envisioned hundred dollar bills bulging from my pockets, and girls clamoring for my attention. Actually, I didn't care about girls in the plural. I wanted only to gain the affection of one: Samantha Blake.

I'd been harboring a crush on Samantha better than a year, but given her elevated stature in the halls of Caprock High School, I'd never acted upon my infatuation. Samantha was a cheerleader; I was a cowboy boot-wearing rabbit raiser. She was graceful, petite, and beautiful; I was a six-foot-three sophomore who hadn't quite mastered the coordination of my man-sized body. She was one of the most popular girls at our high school; I'd lost my bid to become FFA president.

Turns out not even Scott, my best friend, voted for me. Not that I blame him. After all, my opponent to head up Caprock High's Future Farmers of America was Destiny Hayes. Destiny had been wildly popular with all of the guys since the fourth grade, when she was the first girl to grow a set of boobs. Then there we were in high school, and the other girls had yet to make up for Destiny's head start. Scott had been in love with her, or at least her bra size, since elementary school, but as I said, there was only one girl for me.

Samantha Blake wasn't like the superficial and pretentious cheerleaders in movies. She was sweet, kind, and possessed long, black eyelashes that left me tongue-tied every time they fluttered in my presence. Scott maintained that other girls in our class were just as pretty. A point I might have conceded, except . . . none of those other girls made my heart accelerate with a single word. None of them made me lie awake at night, thinking about their big brown eyes.

None of them were Samantha Blake. Okay, so it wasn't her eyes I stayed up at night pondering. My thoughts were of a more libidinous and lusty nature. I was a teenage boy, after all. Nevertheless, my sleepless nights and unacknowledged attraction for Samantha paled in comparison to my boss's brand of lady troubles.

Doyle had three women in his life. His first wife and the mother of his three boys, Pamela. His second wife, Laura, whom he was in the process of divorcing when I hired on, and last, but not least, Snuggles.

Snuggles was an English Bulldog. Brown and white, she was one of the laziest, not to mention nastiest, canines to ever down a bowl of kibble. Snuggles possessed runny, pus-filled eyes, a loud, raspy breathing pattern reminiscent of an asthmatic Darth Vader, and stubby, bowed legs that barely kept her flabby gut from dragging the ground. She also happened to be Doyle's most prized possession.

Ninety percent of the time, Snuggles curled up on her doggy bed behind the counter and refused to move. Too bad for me if I needed something from the cabinet her fat body was pressed against. Once or twice per day she would hoist her smelly carcass from the fleece pad, only to use my pant leg as a depository for her snot-crusted eyes. Nasty to be sure, but that act beat her other habit all to hell.

Doyle lived for the times when Snuggles went into heat. Having read an ad in the Thrifty Nickel for English Bulldog pups fetching thirteen-hundred bucks a pop, mining Snuggles' ovaries became his life's mission. I, however, dreaded the arrival of the dog's cycle. For this glorious week, Snuggles wasn't merely content to wipe her eye boogers on my jeans. No—she also felt the animalistic calling to drag her butt across the store's concrete floor.

Guess who cleaned up the crimson snail trails. Me.

The only good thing about these visits from Mother Nature was the entertainment they provided at each failed attempt by Doyle to produce a litter of grandpups. Doyle whored Snuggles out to every male bulldog within a three-county area. Too greedy to share in the potential booty of a litter worth several grand, Doyle opted to pay up-front stud fees rather than give up a higher share should she actually conceive.

For each arranged rendezvous, Snuggles would shack up with the chosen doggy Don Juan. Three or four days later she'd return from her tryst looking as happy and satisfied as a fat man leaving a Vegas buffet. Given the price of bulldog pups, Doyle projected Snuggles and her uterus to be good for an easy five grand per year, and by his calculations, she only needed to have two litters of two pups to accomplish that goal.

Along with the dog, Doyle was also raising three boys. Three mean little hoodlums that I wagered would make him a grandpa long before Snuggles ever did. Never mind the fact that Austin, the oldest, was only eleven. Their father's genes were too strong for them not to find trouble of some sort, and given Doyle's track record, some of that trouble was bound to be of the female variety.

To this day I still can't fathom how Doyle sweet-talked so many women into the sack.

When pimping out Snuggles failed to work, Doyle turned to artificial insemination. The procedure was pricey, but each time Snuggles came into heat, he'd reach for his credit card, load the pooch into his pickup, and head for the vet's.

Then came the day I was in the back, sacking up hen scratch for Mrs. Esparza. Doyle had taught me how to upsell, so I was in the middle of trying to convince the woman a bit of oyster shell and a bag of laying pellets would raise her egg production.

"As hens get older," I said, "they really need the extra calcium they gain from oyster shells."

"No, no, no. *No hay falta con mis gallinas.*" Mrs. Esparza wagged a finger in my face. She was a regular customer, so I knew my chances of selling her anything extra were over once she slipped back to Spanish. Next she would pretend not to understand anything I said.

"Yo, Travis!" Doyle's voice ran out on the intercom, saving me from continuing what would have been a futile effort.

"Yeah!" I yelled back.

"Hurry up and get Mrs. Esparza loaded. I have a mission for you."

I carried the hen scratch out, loaded it in Mrs. Esparza's

Buick, and headed back inside to see what Doyle had in mind.

"John's bringing some papers by for me to sign, so I need you to take Snuggles in for her AI appointment."

John was Doyle's lawyer. Between the divorces, the subpoena for when Doyle's bookie got popped, and other brushes with the justice system, they had a close working relationship, so I didn't think anything of this explanation.

"Okay, but I'm taking your truck. I don't want your dog wiping eye snot on my seats." My pickup had been a recent gift from my grandfather, and despite the '76 Ford's battered appearance and age, I was quite proud of the vehicle. Grabbing the keys for the store's flatbed Ford off the pegboard, I snapped a leash on Snuggles and drug her fat butt out the door.

On the way, Snuggles tried to lay her head on my lap. I managed to fend her off, though I very nearly rear ended a VW bus in the process. Then, right as I turned into the vet's, Snuggles sneezed and blew mucous all over the right side of my face and the driver's window.

Cursing, I reached for a stained Taco Bell napkin on the dash. The lone scrap did little more than smear the snot, so I searched for something else to clean my cheek while Snuggles looked on with smug satisfaction. When I leaned across to open the glove box, the foul beast mistook the gesture as a sign of love and planted her wide, pink tongue on my cheek. The lick left a string of dog slobber oozing from my ear.

In between heartfelt expletives, I wiped the slime off with the back of my hand and headed inside.

Behind the receptionist desk sat a stunning young woman in her early twenties. "Snuggles!" She beamed and came around the counter to pat the dog's head.

Sucking in my stomach, I swelled my chest and proudly said, "She's a good dog."

"She sure is," the girl cooed. Then she looked up at me and frowned. Pointing with a cute, manicured fingernail, the receptionist said, "You've got something on your eyebrow."

Reaching up, I grabbed a gooey green wad of bulldog boogers.

So much for a favorable first impression.

The girl led me and Snuggles back to a waiting room where she left us alone.

Up until then, I'd assumed bulldog semen came in little vials. I assumed they kept it frozen and had a machine that heated it up to the right temperature when needed. I assumed the procedure involved something resembling a turkey baster. Two out of three of my assumptions proved flat-ass wrong.

Dr. Croft came in after only a few minutes and the truth didn't dawn on me even as she bent to lift the bulldog that had followed her into the room. Brutus was his name, as I'd later find out.

I watched the doctor, an attractive woman in her forties, reach beneath the male bulldog, snapp what looked like a sandwich bag around his junk, and begin the collection process.

Like a fan at Wimbledon, my head went back and forth as Dr. Croft established a steady rhythm.

Blood rushed to my cheeks when she looked me in the eye and said, "So you work for Doyle? That must be interesting."

I might have managed a nod as she stroked Brutus. Beside me, Snuggles ignored the poochie porn show. There I was, a teenage boy, trapped in a tiny room, and forced to bear witness as an attractive and secure middle-aged woman jacked off a very well-endowed beast. Most would describe that as interesting.

Not me. I found it mortifying.

Puberty had hit me like a two-ton rock so I had both an active, fantasy-filled imagination and a strong libido, but none of my daydreams had ever starred the canine equivalent of Ron Jeremy. Though I was pretty sure a few of my nightmares were about to. Still, I couldn't look away.

Grimacing, I watched the piston-like movement with held breath and tensed jaw. When the big moment arrived, I actually flinched. Brutus shuddered once, before casually looking over his shoulder as if challenging me to do better. Right about then, I felt as confident as a major leaguer swinging a toothpick.

The only part of the act I'd envisioned correctly was the turkey baster. When the whole sordid event was finished, I'm not sure who felt more violated, me or Snuggles. On the way out I didn't even slow down. No way did I want to chance making eye contact with that pretty receptionist.

Back at the feed store, I slinked in to find Doyle displaying a huge shit-eating grin.

"You could've warned me," I said.

"I could've," he nodded, "but that wouldn't have been nearly as much fun." Doyle laughed, before adding, "Heard you turned redder than Brutus's dipstick."

"What did you want me to do? Cheer the vet on? Offer to lend a hand?"

He shrugged. "You could've volunteered to go next."

"That woulda gone over well."

Doyle served up a lop-sided grin and shrugged. "Worked for me."

Gape-mouthed, I stared.

"Sometimes all you've got to do is ask," Doyle said with a wink and an evil chuckle.

Who knows whether Doyle was telling the truth or just jerking my chain, so to speak, but he taught me a valuable lesson: *Until you're brave enough to ask the question, you'll never hear a yes.*

I could tell you that the whole bulldog experience gave me the confidence to march right up to Samantha Blake and ask her out. Yeah, I could tell you that, but it'd be a lie. Truth is it took many more lessons. Some painful, some criminal, and some downright immoral before I emerged from the feed store a wiser member of the male species.

Perhaps I would've found love without Doyle's depraved guidance. Perhaps, I would've sailed through my teen years and into adulthood unscathed and equally as prepared to face the world. Perhaps, but the ride wouldn't have been nearly as much fun.

Chapter Two

The Perilous Flight

At school I was a near straight A student, but when it came to learning the ways of the world and becoming as bold and confident as my boss, you might say I was a slow learner.

Matter of fact, up to that point in my life, I'd only done one truly bold thing—stolen my job at the feed store. That's right, I thieved the position from Hunter Tomkins, and as blatantly as a pickpocket lifts your wallet. Hunter never even knew he'd been victimized until it was too late, but before I can tell you how I landed my gig at Pearl's Feed and Seed, I first need to reveal a few things about my family.

Noah had nothing on my kinfolk. For every two animals he hauled on his ark, my family raised three. Sure, Noah's cargo was more diverse, but my clan made up for variety through sheer volume. Some critters we raised for show, others simply to fill our meat-loving bellies. Pigs, chickens, dogs, RABBITS. Pigeons, goats, ducks, RABBITS. Geese, donkeys, sheep, and yes, more RABBITS. We never raised cattle or horses, as they required ample acreage and a tidy sum of money, two things my family never possessed. Having said that, I need not explain why I'd been a customer of Pearl's Feed and Seed since the days when the namesake ran the joint.

Back then, Pearl sold not only grain, animal supplies, and assorted lawn and garden paraphernalia, but also wedding, prom, and formal dresses. Pearl was a talented seamstress, and in an odd combo, she operated a custom dress shop from the back half of the feed store. Fancy lace sat mere feet from cucumber seeds. Bolts of satiny fabric hung beside stacks of tomato cages. Headless mannequins stood guard near sacks of cow manure. I'd never had call to purchase a fancy dress, but I grew up visiting the store every few weeks for things like rabbit pellets, fly paper, and chicken scratch. But as I said, Pearl had long abandoned both the store and her sewing operation by the time I stole my job.

Buck Suggs owned Pearl's Feed and Seed. He'd bought the place for his wife Pearl, but after they divorced he turned over the operation to his youngest son, Doyle. Buck owned another feed store as well. A place called Gold Brothers. Gold Brothers had a higher income and a better class of clientele than Pearl's. Buck ran Gold Brothers and his skill and knowledge made that business a success. He'd worked there all of his life and had bought the place from the founding family, thus the name Gold Brothers, rather than Suggs Brothers. Few, if any, knew as much about the local fauna and flora as Buck Suggs. He also possessed the personality and people skills necessary to please virtually every customer who walked through the door.

Doyle had inherited all of Buck's charm, but little of his knowledge. He made up for lack of know-how with an uncanny ability to bullshit. He was the kind of guy you dreaded seeing right up until you were with him. Then you found yourself having such a good time, you forgot your original trepidation. Or at least you did until all that fun caught up to you. By then it was always too late. You were in too deep to bail. Of course, I didn't know any of that when I first took the job.

To call Hunter Tomkins and myself friends would be stretching the truth. We were classmates first and foremost. Sure, we had a few friends in common, but true pals we were not. Then there was our other link. The one we shared outside of school.

Amarillo is by far the largest city in the region. It serves as the hub of a vast area covering Southwestern Kansas and the Oklahoma and Texas Panhandles, as well as eastern New Mexico. Despite its population of nearly 200,000, Amarillo possesses the feel of a small town a fraction that size. The so-called six degrees of separation does not apply to the city's life-long residents.

Two degrees. That's about all you get. Expect more, and you're delusional. Don't believe me?

Have an affair. Be a deacon at First Baptist Church and try to sneak a quick trip to the liquor store. Wreck your car while wearing your wife's red fishnet stockings. No social crime goes unpunished in a town like Amarillo. Everyone gets outed eventually. I even know a fellow unlucky enough to solicit his brother's mother-in-law, who happened to be an undercover cop. Talk about awkward holiday get-togethers.

But back to the connection between Hunter and myself. For years my uncle carried on a honky-tonk love affair. Sure enough, the odds finally caught up to him. Or perhaps his trouble stemmed from hanging around all those prolific bunnies. Either way, he and this woman, the other party in his bar room love affair, conceived a child together. They never married, but since their kid was my cousin, I sometimes hung out over at her house. And my uncle's girlfriend/my cousin's mother just happened to be Hunter Tomkin's godmother.

Why anyone would choose a woman who hangs out in smoky honky tonks getting impregnated by a two-stepping, rabbit-raising Romeo as the source of religious guidance for their child is another matter, and one I won't attempt to explain. Nevertheless, Hunter and I had been thrown together a few times over the years.

One of those occasions found us at Pearl's Feed and Seed. Not at the hands of our families, but at the request of our high school FFA teacher. As part of our agricultural sciences class, we cared for the animals on the school farm, and on a cold and windy March day, our class arrived at said farm only to find the show lambs in bad shape.

A dog had gotten into the enclosure and chased the animals for some time. One was dead. The others had gashes and cuts on their bodies from their panicked flight. So the teacher sent Hunter and me to fetch some Corona (the antiseptic animal ointment, not the Mexican beer) and catgut to sew the animals back together.

There we were, talking to Doyle, when Hunter opened his mouth and said, "Are you hiring? I need a job, and it would be bad-ass to work here."

I don't know what overcame me. Maybe it was the sun streaking through the fly-specked window. Or the dust motes floating lazily around Doyle's head. Heck, maybe it was just the fact I didn't really like Hunter Tomkins, but for whatever reason, a compulsion hit me. "Doyle already promised to hire me," I blurted. As if willing him to go along with my lie, I stared Doyle straight in the eye. "Didn't you?"

The corner of Doyle's lip curled upward in a smile. Winking at me, he said, "Yes, I did. Travis starts Saturday morning at seven-thirty."

Doyle later confessed he hadn't really needed to hire more help, but he'd been impressed by the way I'd cock-blocked Hunter. He also told me my arrival had royally pissed off Jerry, his lone employee before I hit the scene. I soon found out, Doyle enjoyed few things more than annoying those foolish enough to call him boss.

I considered stealing the job from Hunter quite the daring feat, but my theft was nothing compared to one Doyle made shortly after I hired on. Unlike me, Doyle never shied away from conversing with the opposite sex. Matter of fact, he had plenty to say to every woman who entered the feed store, whether they be three or ninety-three. Kids and little old ladies loved him. And he greeted both with a bright smile and kind words. However, the women who fell anywhere in between puberty and social security were often treated to a different side of my boss. Doyle was a master of innuendo. To this day I'm amazed at the things he got away with, but then again, Texas feed stores are not known as parlors of gentlemanly behavior.

In particular, Doyle liked young women, eighteen to twenty-five. I think he felt confident that he could bullshit them without repercussion. When need be, Doyle came across as an all-American decent guy. He could lay on the Eddie Haskell routine without most people realizing they were being had. Let's say a young woman came in to apply for a spring and summer job in the greenhouse. Doyle would always ask the same question. "Do you know how to plant tulips?"

A "yes," and he'd reply with, "Good. I like a woman who knows were to plant her two lips." A "no" would bring out, "Don't worry about it. I've taught more than one woman how to plant two lips." Most never picked up on his comments. Some did, and more than a few eventually took him up on the lessons. There are plenty of stories about Doyle's sexual prowess to come, but for now I simply want you to understand he was a man willing to do most anything to achieve his goals.

As I said, Doyle didn't own the feed store. His dad, Buck, did. The crew that worked over at Gold Brothers didn't have nearly as much fun as we did at Pearl's, but then again they were too busy making actual money to engage in Doyle's brand of misbehavior.

Since a lot of our patrons were elderly and relied on Social Security, or were poor and only had money at the first of the month when their government checks arrived, Doyle let customers charge. We pinned all of the outstanding accounts on a large corkboard behind the cash register. Often there would be ten grand worth of unpaid bills tacked up there, and on occasion Doyle's dad tallied up the board. The sum of which always led to the elder Suggs having a conniption. At which point, Doyle would come under the gun to bring the total down to a more reasonable number.

One of the boss's good friends, Hopalong, had a prosthetic leg from the knee down. Now before you accuse me of being cruel or of making fun of the handicapped, let me say "Hopalong" was what most everybody called him, and if the name bothered him, he never let on. Matter of fact, "Hopalong" was a heck of a lot nicer than what Doyle tended to call the man. And they were the best of friends.

Hopalong's account often swelled to four or five hundred dollars. Mostly due to the expensive grain he purchased for his fighting cocks. On one such occasion, when Buck was raising hell about the charge board, Hopalong's account just happened to be at the half-a-grand mark. The single largest balance on the board, and Buck was after Doyle to collect. Doyle called or drove by his buddy's house every day, but always arrived back at the feed store to report the same answer from Hoppie: "Can't give you what I don't have."

Under pressure, Doyle couldn't give up, so he waited until the third or fourth day of the next month, when Hoppie was scheduled to receive his disability check. Doyle went to the door and knocked. Hopalong's wife let my boss inside. So far so good, but his friend was in the shower. When Doyle called through the bathroom door, Hoppie claimed he still didn't have any money. That's when Doyle spied the plastic leg propped alongside Hopalong's favorite recliner. With the man's wife off in the kitchen fixing him a glass of iced tea, Doyle snatched up the prosthetic leg and hauled it back to the feed store.

Grinning like a drunken pirate, my boss came into the store with the plundered booty tucked beneath his arm. "The son of a bitch will have to pay me now." He stood the plastic limb in the corner behind the counter, and regaled me with the details of his daring heist.

For the next several weeks the leg became the focal point of his jokes. If a customer complained about prices, Doyle reached for the prosthetic. Hoisting it high, he would say, "Tell me about it. Grain costs an arm and a leg these days." Or if someone called bullshit on one of his stories, Doyle would grab the thing and say, "Swear to God, I'm not pulling your leg."

Yep, Doyle got a lot of mileage from the hijacked appendage, but the thing gave me the creeps. It wasn't a new bright and shiny leg, but an old, battered and stained contraption. The once flesh-toned skin possessed a freaky green tint. And I'm not saying it stunk, but flies tended to circle over the prosthetic like buzzards above carrion.

Needless to say, I was glad when Hopalong finally came to fetch the damned thing. He arrived on crutches, with the right pant leg of his jeans safety pinned up. Grinning, he leaned against the counter and dug out his wallet. "Alright cocksucker," he said, slapping cash down on the wood. "Give me back my fucking leg."

Doyle scooped up the money, counted it, and then tossed the leg up on the counter, where it landed with a hollow thunk. "Pleasure doing business with you," he said as Hoppie snapped the limb into place. That night the two of them went to a dive bar over on Amarillo Boulevard, got drunk, and were arrested for public intox and driving under the influence.

I haven't seen Hunter in years, but if Hopalong can forgive his best friend for stealing his leg, surely Hunter can forgive me for stealing a job. Though if I'm being truthful, that job at the feed store wasn't the last thing I thieved from Hunter Tomkins.

Chapter Three

A Leg To Stand On

Pearl's Feed and Seed occupied a nondescript wood building. Two large windows, one on each side of the front door, faced the street, but the glass was dirty and fly-specked, so the resulting light did little to brighten the dusty interior.

To the people who congregated and lingered inside the store, Doyle's presence made up for the complete lack of feng shui. Sure, they came to buy grain and garden supplies, but they stayed to listen to the boss's rants, ramblings, and recitations.

While Doyle held court his audience played cards, pitched quarters, and sipped rancid coffee. They ate the free peanuts Doyle kept on the counter, and listened to diatribes on everything from politics and religion on down to the tight ass on the Mexican girl who worked at the liquor store around the corner.

Some customers came in, purchased their items and left, but many lingered. Every bit as much hangout as place of business, Pearl's was the redneck equivalent of Starbucks.

However, our coffee was the kind of dark, smelly fare that only men would drink, and I'm pretty sure they only drank it to prove the potency of their testosterone. I'm talking about the kind of coffee that makes a person growl after every swallow. The kind of coffee that grows gills when left on overnight. Or sprouts legs over a long weekend. The kind of coffee that Darwin loves, and theologians fear. Never mind putting hair on your chest, the feed store java put hair on your tongue. I wasn't tough enough to actually swallow the brew, but on occasion I'd pour myself a mug and stand around trying to act manly.

The coffee pot sat on a small table near the counter line. Above it hung various tack—bridles, bits, and reins. Two other walls were lined with brown glass bottles full of pesticides, fertilizers, and other assorted chemicals. In the center of the room sat a double-sided shelving unit stocked with various animal supplies, such as medicines, feeders, and show apparatus. A couple of barstools sat up near the counter, providing a spot for Doyle's audience to congregate. The stools were nearly always occupied.

Rusty, the cable man, would sit for hours. In between sips of coffee, he'd puff away on Marlboros while somewhere in town, someone waited not-so-patiently for him to install their HBO. On any given day, you might find Hopalong occupying the stool beside Rusty, unless of course he happened to be behind on his charge account.

Another day it would be Dirty Dick Murdoch, a professional wrestler of substantial girth and even greater bullshitting capacity. Dirty Dick hung about telling lies and bragging about his wild adventures. His stories of the wrestling circuit were entertaining enough, but the wrestler's habit of spitting tobacco juice on the floor was not. Especially given I was the one to mop up.

Sometimes fellow pro wrestler and part-time movie actor, Terry Funk, joined Dirty Dick. Luckily The Funkster was a real man and swallowed his Skoal-tainted saliva. Both men considered themselves ranchers as well as genuine professional athletes.

Then there was Jimmy Bluejacket—a fella who made his living stealing wooden pallets from behind various grocery stores and freight companies, only to sell them to businesses on the other side of town. Jimmy claimed to be kin to the legendary Comanche chief, Quanah Parker. With his dark complexion and high, smooth cheekbones, he sure enough looked the part, and ironically, years later Jimmy ended up behind bars at a state prison down near Quanah, Texas. After the pallet business failed to make him rich, Jimmy became a chemist of sorts, but his illegal meth lab, along with his freedom, went up in smoke when he accidentally burnt down both his house, and the one next door.

All told there were probably two dozen regulars that hung out at Pearl's. But don't think all of them were rough and tumble men. We also had our share of women who perched at the counter line eager to hear Doyle's every word.

Tasha was a newlywed. A horse lover with a face that resembled Doyle's dog, Snuggles, Tasha had the broad shoulders of an NFL linebacker, the bouncy blond curls of Miss Piggy, and the man-hating disposition of a lesbian feminist. Never did I hear her utter a single kind word about a member of the male species, including her brand new husband. The lone exception being Doyle. She would sit for hours and hang on his every word, making sure to bat her clumpy black lashes every time he glanced her way.

Ginger, on the other hand, was a pleasant and nice-looking woman in her early forties. An artist who sold enough paintings to scratch out a living. And she seemed to have read every book ever written. Even back then I was an avid reader, so she and I often discussed books. Ginger was also one of the few who could effectively debate Doyle on just about any subject. But don't let that fool you, she was every bit as batshit crazy as the others who hung out at Pearl's. Ginger's normal side was negated by her over-the-top love for a goat named Wagner.

Wagner was a newborn when I first hired on, and Ginger would come in with the goat swaddled in a frilly, blue baby blanket. She fed him from a bottle and cooed over the furry-faced critter as if he'd crawled out of her womb that very morning. Wagner went everywhere she did. Even after he grew to be a full-sized Billy goat.

Wagner had his own mobile room in the camper-top of her pickup, which was lined bottom, top, and sides with pumpkin-colored shag carpet. According to Ginger, Wagner liked the way it felt beneath his hooves. Of course, she also swore *The Golden Girls* was his favorite TV show.

Also hanging around the feed store would be whatever wife or girlfriend Doyle happened to have at the time, since he wasn't the type of guy women trusted with unchecked freedom.

The good, the bad, and the crazy. That pretty much summed up our clientele. Funny thing is, I have a hard time recalling the good. They came, they paid their bills, and they went. The bad, the crazy—the people who linger in my mind—are the ones who shaped my formative years.

Seven-thirty to six. Monday through Saturday. Those were our hours of operation. I worked pretty much every hour I wasn't in school. Truthfully, I did it as much for the camaraderie, and for the chance to be near so many wonderfully weird and wildly eccentric people, as I did for a paycheck.

I described the front part of the feed store, the space where everyone congregated, but Pearl's had more to it than that. In back, a large warehouse-type area housed the bags of fertilizer, pesticides, animal cages, seed bins, and other large items. This is where Pearl once operated a dress shop. Fabric, mannequins, and various catalogs of patterns still cluttered the far corner. Doyle had turned what once were the fitting and dressing rooms into a small office.

Beyond the warehouse, through a vertical garage door, sat

an outdoor area with a greenhouse and an adjacent fenced in area for chickens, ducks, goats, geese, and any other critters Doyle could resell for a profit. Off to the side of the big back room, was a long slender bunkhouse where we kept the animal feed, as well as the bulk grain.

And then there was my least favorite part of the feed store. Barely bigger than a large closet, the chick room as we called it, held our baby chicks, ducklings, goslings, and parakeets. Poorly ventilated, the tightly confined area smelled horrible. I cleaned it twice a day, every day, but that did little to help the smell or the plethora of maggots that continually hatched in the shit-filled trays beneath the cages. The contents of those trays prevented me from eating rice for a good decade beyond my tenure at Pearl's.

Aside from my baby duck dookie duties—say that three times fast!—I truly liked my job. All except for two days a month. The every-other-Saturday when Doyle brought his three sons in with him. At eleven, Austin was the oldest, and the only skinny one of the bunch. Despite his bony physique, his age and cunning automatically made him the ringleader of the gang. Dallas was nearly as big as his older brother, despite being only eight. As ornery and mean as his older sibling, he lacked the wisdom and experience to truly be dangerous. Houston was Doyle's baby boy. Actually he was a mere ten months younger than Dallas. Nevertheless, when I first went to work at Pearl's, he still possessed a touch of the innocence you often find in seven-year-old boys. However, it wasn't long until his hooligan older brothers beat that naivety right out of him. Like their dad, the boys taught me many valuable lessons, and the first came only a few weeks into my employment at Pearl's Feed and Seed.

It was spring break. I was sixteen, a sophomore, and for the first time in my life held the freedom of a driver's license. Unfortunately, having a set of wheels meant little since I was scheduled to work every day of my school vacation. Seven-thirty in the morning 'til six in the evening. All because the feed store's lone employee, besides myself and Doyle, had decided to take the week off.

Jerry Greer hated me from day one.

A goofy little Barney Fife type of guy, Jerry took his job way too serious. With my hiring, Doyle bestowed upon him the title of Warehouse Manager, which made Jerry consider himself my boss. My title was Assistant Warehouse Manager, which would have given credibility to Jerry's belief, except Doyle told me not to listen to anything Jerry said. Jerry resented me for a million different reasons, and I'm fairly certain he took that week off just to make certain I worked all of spring break.

He claimed to be headed for his mother's place in Arkansas, but Doyle dismissed that as a lie. He said people like Jerry were hatched in an incubator and had no clue who their mother was. Doyle insisted Jerry would spend the entire week on his couch, drinking room-temperature cans of Busch beer while his herd of house cats looked on, waiting for him to puke so they would have something to eat. The mental image of that scene was nearly as painful as working all of spring break. Making matters worse, Doyle's three sons were also out of school, and that meant they, too, were trapped at Pearl's for the duration of the week.

Throwing a football in the greenhouse, they knocked over a pallet loaded with flats of tomato seedlings, forcing me to spend one whole afternoon replanting the tiny green shoots. Playing king-of-the-hill, the boys destroyed fifteen or twenty sacks of grain, which I spent several dusty hours rebagging. And one evening, unbeknownst to Doyle or me, they left open the door to the parakeet cage.

Early the next morning we discovered five or six dozen of the colorful little birds flitting around the store. The sight was somewhat cool, until I spotted the tiny white flecks of parakeet poop covering every surface like a fine dusting of snow.

By noon, all but a few of the birds had been caught, and most of the droppings had been cleaned. The boys continued to occupy themselves trying to recapture the few remaining escapees. Doyle urged them on, even after Austin knocked over and shattered a thirty-dollar bottle of pesticide. Of course, he wasn't the one forced to clean the resulting mess or shards of glass.

One particular parakeet, a sky-blue and white one, continued to elude them. Swooping in low over their heads, it seemed to almost dare the boys. The tiny little bird dived and fluttered about, always staying just beyond reach.

I was torn.

On one hand, I enjoyed seeing the underdog bird savoring his freedom and denying satisfaction to Doyle and his three heathen offspring. On the other, I knew they would never give up. Regardless of the carnage created by the chase.

And then it happened.

Like a Boeing DC-9 on approach to DFW, the little-blue-bird-that-could soared in low over Dallas's head. The middle son lunged with a makeshift net created from a clothes hanger and an onion sack. He missed his target but managed to clip the bird and disrupt its flight path. With a tiny thud, the parakeet crash landed into the front window and disappeared behind the display of fly paper. Houston was the first to run over and find the damaged creature. He picked it up, but it was obvious the plate glass had taken a serious toll. The parakeet's head was cocked at a painful angle, and one wing hung limply to the side. Doyle took the bird from his youngest son's hand, gave its tiny neck a quick twist to put the suffering to an end, and then unceremoniously tossed the carcass in the trashcan. Only now there were two pieces. The body, and the head.

Seemingly unaffected, the boys shrugged and took off to demolish something else. Doyle grabbed the sports section and headed to the bathroom, and I stayed up front to watch for customers. The little bird lay dead and forgotten in the waste basket.

Hours later, I walked into the back room to sack up a

couple of pounds of thick-bladed fescue seed. Out of the corner of my eye, I spied Houston playing with something. His older brothers had disappeared, yet he was talking away as if someone were there beside him. That's when I noticed something blue in each of his grubby little hands. Squinting to see what he had, it took me a few seconds to recognize the dead parakeet. Houston held the body in one hand and the head in the other as he created a dialog between the two.

Handing the customer his sack of grass seed, I heard Doyle say, "Quit playing with that damn bird and throw it in the trash where it belongs."

The week dragged on and I gave no more thought to the little blue bird or its failed escape. Then on Saturday morning, the next to last day of my school vacation, Jerry showed up asking Doyle if he could go ahead and work.

The boss chewed on the corner of his mustache and said, "I thought you were going to spend the week with your mom over in Fayetteville."

Jerry ran a hand through his mop of black hair, "I got tired of her bitching and came back early."

"Bullshit," Doyle said, "you ran out of beer money."

Jerry didn't admit the other man was right, but he conceded the point by saying, "I need to charge some cat food, too."

"And next you'll wanna bum a smoke," Doyle said.

"Can I?"

"Grab a pack," the boss pointed at the freezer, "I'll add it to your account."

Since he pocketed the money and didn't share it with his dad, Doyle earned as much from selling cigarettes from the freezer, and soda from the fridge, as he did peddling the store's regular wares.

Swinging open the freezer door, Jerry reached inside for a pack of cancer sticks. "What the hell?" He pulled out a crumpled blue ball—the frozen carcass of the parakeet. Somehow, the head was reattached.

"What kind of sick motherfucker sticks a parakeet in the freezer?" Jerry demanded. He shook the tiny body and as he did, the head rolled off and fell at his feet.

Doyle winked at me as Jerry bent and gingerly picked up the decapitated head. "Damn, Jerry you broke it. Me and the boys were doing an experiment. Their science teacher told them you could freeze a live parakeet. She said once it thawed it would fly off as if it'd never been frozen. But hell no, you gotta come along and rip its head off before we can let it defrost."

"I, uh ..." Jerry stammered. He stared, horror-stricken, at the two pieces in his hand.

Doyle folded his arms across his chest and stared angrily at his employee. "Why'd you shake it so hard?"

"I didn't do it on purpose. You know that. I'm an animal lover. You know me."

"Who gives a shit whether you done it on purpose. What

matters is you killed the thing. I can't sell a dead parakeet. Now you owe me another seven bucks."

Jerry shook his head. "Put it on my account, but I still say only a sick motherfucker would freeze a live animal."

Doyle bit his lower lip to keep from laughing. "You calling my kids motherfuckers?"

Quick to shake his head, Jerry said, "No. But I wouldn't want any kid of mine doing shit like that." Working himself back into a frenzy, he muttered, "I don't give a tinkers damn how many teachers told 'em to."

Doyle let out a low whistle and slowly shook his head. "Actually Jerry, it's probably best you've never had any kids."

"Why's that?"

Shooting me another wink, Doyle answered, "Because I'd hate for you to pass on your genes."

Jerry frowned. Looking down at his stained and tattered Wranglers, he plucked at the blue denim with his free hand. "Why the hell would I give these pants to my kids?"

Doyle and I laughed until tears stained our cheeks. No sooner would we gain our composure then Jerry would ask, "What's so fucking funny?" At which point we'd lose it again.

Turns out the actions of Doyle's wild, destructive sons, combined with the wayward flight of the brave little parakeet-that-couldn't, taught me what no clichéd after-school special or public service announcement ever could: the importance of staying in school.

But my education didn't end there. Not by a long shot. I

can see now that my flight into adulthood was every bit as perilous as that little blue parakeet's, but then again freedom of any type always comes with a price. Learning to fly both out the door and out of the nest is a dangerous, painful, and often embarrassing endeavor that gives credibility to the saying, "No pain, no gain."

Or as Doyle liked to say, *Don't be a puss. Try it ... It'll make a man out of you.*

Chapter Four

Forebber A Field Of Dreams

Not long after the parakeet's fateful flight, the boys were at the store one Saturday afternoon when I overheard the following conversation between Austin and his dad.

"Mom wants to know if you can take Dallas and Houston to Wonderland this Friday. It's 'school' night."

"You're not going?" Doyle never bothered to look up from the newspaper.

"Yeah, I'm goin', but I got a date. And Mom says that means we should go alone."

Doyle folded the paper and tossed it aside. "How about I take you and your date, and she hauls your brothers?"

Austin shrugged. "Fine by me, but Mom said you'd scare her even worse than them."

Father and son kept right on discussing the details. Distracted, I didn't pay much attention. My mind couldn't let go of the fact Austin had a date. He was all of eleven. Here I was sixteen and I'd never so much as asked a girl for her phone number. None of my friends ever took a girl to the amusement park back when our elementary school had Wonderland night. Best as I could recall, my sixth grade buddies and I were more focused on how many times we could ride The Hammer without puking than we were our female classmates. Nevertheless, Austin's revelation unearthed some primal competitive urge within me. Fueled by shame that an eleven-year-old had accomplished what I'd never even attempted, I vowed to at least tie the diminutive Don Juan and have my own date come next Friday.

Returning my attention to the father-son conversation, I heard Doyle ask, "This isn't that same redheaded girl you took to the movies is it?"

So much for my tie. Unless I could fashion my own flux capacitor and track down a silver DeLorean, I was screwed when it came to keeping up with Austin. Nevertheless, somehow, someway, I needed to take a chance and dive into the dating pool. Thoughts of Samantha Blake immediately flooded my mind, but of course I couldn't ask her out. A guy doesn't do a half-gainer into the deep end without knowing how to swim. At least this guy didn't. There were far too many variables for me to make that leap. If Samantha said no, my leaden heart would drag me to the bottom of the pool. On the other hand, she could say yes, but even if that happened I just might drown simply because I had no idea what to do next.

"What's this girl's name?" Doyle asked his son.

"Heather."

Heather. That figured. I went to school with two Heathers. Both hot. No doubt Austin's Heather was the fifth grade equivalent of hot.

Doyle smiled as if he too knew a good looking Heather or two. "What's her mom look like?"

Austin shrugged. "Beats me, but her dad has a Harley."

"New or old?"

"I dunno," Austin said. "New I guess."

Doyle rolled his eyes. "Figures. Probably a damn lawyer. Or doctor. Nobody else can afford a new Harley. What time do you need to go?"

"Sometime after school, I guess."

Doyle nodded. "I'll take off early and pick you up. Travis can stay and close up that day."

"Can't," I said. "I have a date myself."

"With who?" Doyle was always asking about "the chicks" I went to school with and how come I wasn't out chasing them. I'd made the mistake of mentioning Samantha Blake and the fact I was too nervous to ask her out. A fact Doyle had snacked upon like a fat kid with a sack full of cotton candy.

Therefore, I knew he'd have a piss-pot full of questions about my date. But I couldn't tell him what I didn't know myself, so I replied with, "a girl," and high-tailed it back to the feed room before he could ask anything else.

That next Monday, I asked out Darlene Wilshire. A year behind me at Caprock High, Darlene was a pretty little freshman. A quiet, petite girl with big, innocent brown eyes. She sat behind me in second period Latin, and until I stopped her in the hall, we'd never talked about anything more exciting than the proper translation of *vini, vidi, vici*. When asked if she would like to see a movie with me on Friday her eyes widened and, for a few seconds, I thought she might flee by bolting down the hall. But then, maybe as a result of her surprise, she blinked a few times and said, "I'd love to." Easy as that, I had my first honest-to-goodness date. Too bad the easy ended there.

My dad wasn't around much when I was a kid. Not even before he and my mom split. Matter of fact, I can't even say for sure when they divorced. That's how little of an impact the event had on my everyday life. My mom had always been my lone source of parental guidance, but no way was I about to seek dating advice from her. That left only one knowledgeable resource at my disposal—Doyle.

At the time, Doyle was in the midst of his second divorce. That should've given me a clue his expertise on affairs of the heart was a bit flawed. It should have, but didn't. When you're a sixteen-year-old boy with the self-confidence of a plump turkey the day before Thanksgiving, and nowhere else to turn for advice, a duo of failed marriages do not seem nearly as important as the fact two women had once said yes to him.

I'd met Doyle's first wife. She came around fairly often to either pick up the three boys or drop them off, but I'd never laid eyes on Laura, wife number two. My only contact with the woman had been her frequent phone calls to the store. She screamed, hollered, and cussed the second anyone picked up the phone. She didn't even care if Doyle was the one to answer.

He described Laura as the biggest mistake of his life, and given some of the things he'd done, that title came with stiff competition. They say there's a fine line between love and hate. Best I could tell, both Laura and Doyle enjoyed walking that emotional tightrope. Doyle told me he'd picked Laura up in some bar, took her home, and promptly impregnated her. Trying to do the right thing, they traipsed down to the Justice of the Peace and became man and wife. Within a week of saying I do, Doyle realized she was completely bat-shit crazy.

"Crazy is good between the sheets," Doyle liked to say. "But outside the bedroom, crazy ain't nothing but a pain in the ass."

According to the boss, sex with Laura was good enough to make the Pope howl at the moon, but a few months after their nuptials, Laura miscarried. Laura blamed their bedroom antics, whereas Doyle saw it as a sign from God to cut and run while the getting was good. Filing for divorce, Doyle fired the first shot in what proved to be a long war, and even though I wasn't around to hear that first bullet whiz by, I experienced my share of explosions. The angry, expletive-laced phone calls, the threats, the tearful pleas to have Doyle call her because she really did love him. Then Laura commissioned her brother to threaten Doyle. Or maybe it was a cousin. I can't remember for sure but either way, Doyle wasn't the kind of guy that frightened easily.

Next, Laura went for a restraining order. Doyle's lawyer countered and used phone records to prove Laura initiated the repeated contact, and therefore, was the harassing party. All the while, Doyle seemed unfazed. He continued to be his usual laid-back and care-free self. Doyle believed all problems went away if ignored long enough. He dated a few women here and there while his lawyer continued to fight on his behalf.

Then, Laura tried to kill him, but I'm getting ahead of myself. The attempted murder happened long after my first date.

Like I said, Doyle was still in the early stages of his divorce from Laura when I asked Darlene out. A few months down the road, I would've known better, but at the time, it seemed perfectly sane to seek dating advice from Doyle Suggs. Now I couldn't come right out and tell my boss this was to be my first-ever date. No, that would have fueled far too much ridicule on the heels of my confession that I was too scared to ask out Samantha Blake. Playing it cool, I leaned against the front counter and said, "I sure hope my date on Friday works out. She's a freshman and you know what that means."

Doyle's expression said, *No, I don't know what that means.*

Truthfully, neither did I, but I kept right on talking

with the hope I'd find a way to nonchalantly ask for advice. "Chances are she's never even been on a date. What if I'm her first?"

"We still talking about dates?" Doyle winked and added, "Or you telling me you're scared to go cherry pickin'?"

Now he was messing with me. "I'm talking about dates."

"Yeah. But you're thinking about cherries. Ain't you?"

I opened my mouth to speak but Doyle kept right on talking.

"It's all about risk and reward. If this gal's never even been on a date, her daddy is gonna be on high alert. Chances are he'll try to scare you right off the bat. If he tells you something stupid like, 'I've been to prison before, and I ain't scared to go back,' you got nothing to worry about. He's all talk. Same thing if he's sitting around cleaning his guns. But if he just glares at you, and barely says a word, watch your ass. He's dangerous."

"I'm not worried about her dad." That part was true. Matter of fact, I'd barely given the subject any thought. I got along well with most people, and I figured surviving the ten or fifteen minutes with Darlene's parents would be easier than several hours with her if I made a fool of myself. Or the lasting shame around school if I did something especially stupid.

Doyle rolled his eyes. "That's because you're a 'nice guy.'" He used his fingers to suggest quotes. The dismissive tone of his voice made clear his opinion of the term. "Daddies must love you. Hell, you'll probably engage the bastard in a full conversation. I can hear you now, sitting at the family table chatting about fishing, the weather, or some other nonsense. But guess what? The more her daddy likes you, the less likely you are to get in her panties. Girls, especially high school girls, wanna piss off their daddies, so the last thing they wanna do is bring him home a new buddy."

To my naive sixteen-year-old mind, Doyle's explanation made a good bit of sense.

"Show her right up front you don't give a shit what anyone thinks. That you're not afraid to break a few rules. Show her you're a fucking rebel, and she'll be more than willing to show you a few things as well."

I was listening intently, even considering his advice, but the execution of this principle had me a bit perplexed. "So what am I supposed to do? Show up, call Darlene's mom a whore, flip-off her dad, and yank her out to my truck by the roots of her hair?"

"Darlene?" Doyle grinned. "Your date's name is Darlene? Who the hell names their kid Darlene in this day and age? Where's this girl from, Arkansas?"

"No. Mangum, Oklahoma," I fired back since that's where Doyle's family called home.

Doyle laughed. One thing about him, he took jabs every bit as well as he threw them. "Okay, I'm going to help you out and hand over my fool-proof, panty-dropping, first-date advice. But first tell me, where you taking her?"

I shrugged. "Out to eat and the movies, I guess."

The boss shook his head. "God, you do need help. Otherwise poor Darlene is liable to fall flat asleep and dream she's back in Arkansas slopping the hogs. If she suddenly shouts, *Woo Pig Sooie!* you might wanna nudge her so she doesn't miss the end of the movie."

"She's not from Arkansas!" Doyle was starting to irritate me. Even worse, he knew it. Which meant he wasn't likely to stop, unless I got him back on track. "So what's your great first date advice?"

Swelling his chest, he said, "Flowers. Give her flowers."

"Flowers? You give me all that flak about being predictable, and boring, and too nice then you want me to show up at her door with flowers?"

"Who said anything about showing up at her door with 'em." Doyle grinned. "Not me. Anyone can buy flowers. What you gotta do is steal 'em—and let her see you do it." He spent the next half hour instructing me on the perfect heist. The first step was to scout a location. Find a yard in her neighborhood with some pretty blossoms. Not on the same street, but at least one or two away. That way if things went well I wouldn't have to spend future dates worrying about her neighbor recognizing my truck.

No roses, was his second big tip. Doyle claimed to be drawing from experience when he cautioned me about the perils of thorns. He went on to explain how I needed to break the stems just above ground since dirt and roots didn't go along with romance. Winking, he added, "At least not on a first date."

Finally, he wrapped up by saying that flowers were a lot like kisses: All the sweeter when stolen.

Friday came and I had to work until the store closed at six. Which meant I didn't have time to go home, so I changed right there at Pearl's. Luckily, Darlene didn't live far so I had plenty of time to cruise the streets in her neighborhood before picking her up. Spotting a yard with some nice yellow daffodils three streets over, I headed for her house with my heart buzzing like a swarm of killer bees.

Despite Doyle's dire warning, her father didn't greet me with a shotgun in hand. Matter of fact, he didn't greet me at all. He sat on the couch, watching some old black-and-white Western while his wife let me in. Darlene's mom introduced first herself, and then my date's father, but when I stepped his direction to offer my hand, he merely nodded a hello before reaching for the remote. Turning up the volume, he never looked my direction again during the five minutes I stood there, waiting on Darlene to make her appearance. My date finally walked into the room looking as nervous as I felt. We made eye contact for half a second before she said, "I'm ready if you are."

Her mom bid us a lackadaisical farewell and shuffled off to another room before we were even out the door. My gut told me I'd been wrong about Darlene. Judging by her parents' disinterest, she had to have been on dates before.

Heck, for all I knew, she'd been on dozens. My nerves went haywire as we walked to my truck. I was planning to open the passenger door for her, but she threw me off by walking up to the driver's side. When I opened it, Darlene slid half way across and then stopped. Our legs touched when I got in, and suddenly I thought things might work out after all. Leg pressed against leg, we set out.

With my mind on other things, we were several blocks away before I remembered the flowers, but I couldn't go back to my pre-scouted locale now, at least not without looking like a fool. But Doyle had convinced me the only way to make an impression was to burglarize a batch of blossoms. Improvising, I turned into the next residential area and began scouring yards for colorful foliage.

Then I spotted them. An entire patch of bright pink peonies. Jamming my truck into park, I hopped out and jogged across the lush, green lawn.

Behind me, Darlene asked, "What are you doing?"

Focusing on the prized peonies, I didn't respond. Blood pounded in my head as if I were about to rob a bank. Over the course of the week, I'd convinced myself stealing flowers really wasn't a big deal. After all, they would soon grow back. But now, in the midst of the act, I was anxious. Like a pickpocket at the policeman's ball.

The peonies were planted in a whiskey barrel right up next to the porch.

I glanced at the front door.

Open.

Somebody was home, but I couldn't chicken out now. And then I was there, with my hands on the little green stems. One snap, two snap, and suddenly I had a handful of blooms.

My heart soared. The nervousness eased.

I turned to head back to my truck. Smiling at Darlene, I held up my prize and jogged her direction.

Eyes wide in obvious wonder, she gazed back. Not for an instant did I let my eyes drift from hers.

Victory mine, I was halfway back to the truck when my toe hooked the garden hose stretched across the lawn. Before the triumphant smile even left my face, I was nose-down with a mouth full of wet Bermuda.

An excited little, "Oh," escaped Darlene, which motivated me to hop up and act like I'd planned to plant my kisser smack dab in the soggy turf.

Reaching the truck, I handed her the flowers. One stem had broken in the fall, and most of the petals had been jarred loose, but I'll give Darlene credit, she took them without laughing. Though I'm fairly certain she bit her lower lip to keep from it. The knees of my jeans were wet and stained from the water-soaked lawn, and all through dinner my left elbow throbbed.

After our meal, I drove us to the movie theater where we watched Kevin Costner build a baseball diamond in the middle of a cornfield. A quite appropriate choice given the knees of my Wranglers were grass-stained like those of a diving left fielder.

A few years back I hopped in a cab while in Vegas and proceeded to get a lecture from the driver. In a thick, Greek accent, the man cautioned me to never gamble so much as a single dollar. Seeing as how he'd just picked me up under the awning at The Flamingo, and we were en route to The Golden Nugget, he should have realized I surely represented a lost cause when it came to gambling, but that didn't prevent him from speaking his mind.

"Bet one dollar and win and chew will forebber be gambler. What chew are and what chew like all determined by first taste," he said. "Win once, and chew fool yourself into thinking you can do it over and over again."

It would be easy to discount him and his philosophy as amateur psychology at its worst, but I have to admit that to this day I have a powerful aversion to both peonies and thievery. That Greek cabdriver just might have unearthed one of life's few answers.

Perhaps, I would be a different person had Doyle's scheme produced better results. Perhaps that water hose saved me from a life of crime. Perhaps I would have wound up doing time alongside Doyle's pal, Jimmy Bluejacket. H for manufacturing meth, me for flower piracy.

I'm not saying being friends with Doyle carried a mandatory prison sentence, but then again, it wasn't exactly a Field of Dreams either.

Chapter Five

Even If It Kills You

Darlene and I went out a few more times before discovering the common ability to translate and diagram Latin sentences was not the basis of a great and lasting relationship. We parted as friends and I'll always be grateful to her for one thing—never breathing a word about my pathetic attempt to steal flowers for her. At least I assume she never revealed my stupidity since no one at school ever teased me about the incident. The halls of Caprock High, like those of every other high school in America, were far from being the bastion of sympathetic compassion or undue kindness, so no doubt she kept the secret at least until I graduated and moved on. Until now I've never told anyone either, including Doyle, but I feel confident none of you will tell. Surely you can keep a secret at least as well as Darlene Wilshire.

My sophomore year came to an unspectacular end, and three weeks into summer break, my part-time job at Pearl's became full-time when Jerry wrapped his jalopy of a station wagon around a telephone pole. The collision didn't hurt

Jerry, but he had a blood alcohol level higher than his IQ score and half a dozen unpaid tickets in his file. Therefore, Jerry was forced to settle his debt to the county by serving seventy-some-odd days in the gray bar hotel.

Doyle wasn't about to do all the heavy lifting by himself, so easy as that, I got promoted to Warehouse Manager. The title came with a thirtycent per-hour raise and unlimited access to the company gym. By "gym" I don't mean a place full of free weights, Nautilus equipment, and treadmills. No, I mean a sweltering hot feed room with an unlimited and steady supply of cumbersome grain sacks, heavy mineral blocks, and back-breaking hay bales. Never mind the fact that there wasn't a scrap of spandex or an aerobic class in sight, that summer transformed my body quicker than you can say anabolic steroid. Each week I stacked and unstacked in excess of fifty tons' worth of animal feed. My shoulders broadened, my biceps grew, and my stomach tightened. But despite the newfound brawn of my body, I remained that same, unsure boy.

Doyle on the other hand had an overabundance of confidence which spilled forth every time he opened his mouth. He must have had a million sayings he liked to routinely spout. But his all-time favorite, and the one that most often comes to my mind when thinking of him, was, "Say what you mean, mean what you say." Doyle followed his own advice by doing both. Even when discretion and subtlety would have been the better and more obvious choice.

Another of his often-said lines was, "Confucius say, man

with hole in pocket, feel cocky." Suffice to say, Doyle's pockets were holier than Billy Graham and Mother Teresa combined. Doyle didn't simply feel cocky, he had a stranglehold on cocky. He grabbed it with both hands, stroked it, and shouted, "Danger! I piss on thee." Metaphorically speaking, of course.

Never was this attitude clearer than when Laura tried to kill him.

The first time, it happened on one of those warm summer nights. And yes, I said the *first* time. The kind of night where the stars above gleamed like rhinestones under a spotlight. The kind of night where the moon shines bright and werewolves aren't the only things howling. The kind of night that smooth-talking men, like Doyle, are quick to capitalize on.

That night Doyle found himself at a country bar, a place officially called The Caravan, though most men referred to the honky-tonk as Menopause Manor. An apt moniker given the Caravan's female clientele had seen more hot flashes than Smoky the Bear. Doyle's buddies teased him about picking up old women, but he would simply grin and say, "Mature women need love too. Besides, they never tell, they don't swell, and once the lights go out, they're graceful as hell."

So there he was, leaving the bar on a hot June night after a night of drinking, dancing, and damsel deceiving. A dainty little brunette, ten years his senior, ambled along at his side. They strolled across the pothole-riddled parking lot oblivious to the danger lurking in the shadows.

A car screeched around the corner, only narrowly missing Doyle and his brunette du jour. After the fact, half a dozen witnesses identified Laura, or at least her car. But Doyle never admitted to recognizing his ex, or her vehicle—at least not to the authorities. Then again he was a bit preoccupied with getting out of the way. The brunette pressed charges. Doyle chose not to. A staunch follower of the *No Harm, No Foul* ideology, he wasn't the least bit upset Laura attempted to turn him into road kill. His only regret was that his soon-to-be ex's actions unnerved the brunette to the point that after the police report was filed, she chose to go home alone, rather than allow him to accompany her.

The second time Laura tried to kill him there wasn't near as many witnesses, and the end result proved far more damaging to Doyle's long-term health. You might remember that I said Doyle's pal Jimmy Bluejacket earned his money stealing pallets. A true statement, but in reality, the guy would do just about anything for a buck, regardless of the legality.

Four or five months passed after the nearhit and run. According to Doyle, Laura took some kind of plea bargain for the parking lot incident after the brunette refused to let the matter go. After that, Laura laid low for awhile. She served her probation and community service, and after her divorce from Doyle became final, she finally stopped calling the store.

During that short, but welcome, time of peace, school started back up. I was fortunate enough to have Samantha Blake in two of my classes that junior year. Not that our shared schedule gave me any hope. Over the summer, she'd begun dating a senior. Nevertheless, I sat behind Samantha in both classes, and over the course of the year, we became really good friends. A fact that only strengthened my affection for her.

Fall slipped into winter with nary a word from Laura and then a few days before Christmas, right about my seventeenth birthday, she called and begged Doyle to take her back. Well, she didn't beg him directly, since he screened his calls through me. The list of people he didn't want to talk to grew daily, so I got used to hearing their stories firsthand.

There was the gal he'd once dated in junior high who now wanted to reconnect. Doyle claimed she would first have to pry herself away from the buffet table before he'd be willing to "reconnect." There was the dude Snuggles had bitten and who now wanted Doyle to pay for his medical bills and lost wages. Never mind the fact Doyle had found the bitee lurking in his rural driveway at three in the morning. Sure Snuggles barked at him, but I believed Doyle when he said the bulldog was too lazy to actually bite anybody, even a supposedly lost guy wandering around on dirt roads in the middle of the night. And then there were the plethora of salesmen who called trying to peddle their wares.

I screened them all, so it was me who answered when Laura called that gray December day. Per the routine, I would answer and give Doyle some clue as to who was on the other end.

"Oh hi, LAURA, how are you?"

At the sound of his ex's name Doyle shook his head and made slashing gestures across his throat.

"No, he's not. I'm not really sure when he'll be back. Hard to say. You know how doctors are."

Doyle frowned at my mention of the word doctor.

One of the perks to screening his calls was the opportunity to improvise stories. Stories Doyle was powerless to interrupt unless he wanted to reveal his presence to the person on the other end of the line.

"I'm not really supposed to say," I said. "But just between me and you, he's been having some trouble with little Doyle."

The boss motioned for me to hang up, but I couldn't resist torturing him the way he often did me. Just the idea I'd start a rumor about his favorite appendage riled him.

"No, I don't think he has any of those. I don't think it's a disease at all. Things just aren't working right. Actually, I don't think they're working at—"

Doyle reached over and hung up the phone with his finger.

"What did you do that for?" I asked, handing him the receiver.

"Don't be a jackass," he said. "What did she want?"

"You," I answered. "She told me to tell you she wants you back."

"That'll be a cold day," he mumbled.

Over the course of several days she called dozens of times

and gave me ever-increasing, and ever-embarrassing, messages to pass along.

Tell him I miss him.

Tell him I love him more than anything in this world.

Tell him I'll do anything to win his heart back and to prove how much he means to me.

Tell him he is the water for my thirsty soul and the very memory of his touch on my skin makes me shudder.

Tell him I miss his magic tongue slowly...

Okay, you get the idea. After a while I began to wonder if the two of them were playing a game to see how far along they could push me. Except I detected genuine desperation and longing in her voice.

Then came the gifts.

Flowers one day. Chocolates the next. A racy negligee the third, along with a nasty note of what that scrap of silk and lace could lead to. Doyle was just beginning to get that gleam in his eye, the one he got anytime an attractive, or simply willing, woman walked into the store.

Then, all at once, the calls stopped.

He surmised that her probation had ended and she'd finally given up and moved back north to the tiny Texas Panhandle town where she'd grown up and lived until hooking up with Doyle.

Then, a week or so into the new year, 1990, Ol' Jimmy Bluejacket walked into the store with a two-hundred dollar check drafted on Laura's account.

Doyle took one look and asked, "What are you doing working for Laura? Don't you know she's crazy?"

"Trust me, I know," Jimmy said. He was heavy into drugs by that time, and his front teeth had already started to turn black, so his grin presented an ominous sight. "She paid me to do you in." Jimmy was quick to put up a hand. "But don't worry, I ain't gonna really try. I just want you to cash this for me." He flipped the check over. "I already signed the back."

Never mind the fact Doyle had just heard one of his friends admit he'd taken blood money from his ex-wife. Never mind he was paying out money to his own would-be killer. Never mind somebody wanted him dead. Doyle simply opened the register and counted out ten twenties, which he exchanged for the paper bearing Laura's signature. "Two hundred bucks is all you could get out of her?"

The drug-addled derelict pocketed the cash without bothering to count it. "Nah, that's just the first part. I was supposed to get another three hundred once I finished the job. But like I said, I ain't gonna go after that."

The two talked a while longer as I went back to sweeping the floor. I figured Doyle would call the police, her probation officer, or at the very least his lawyer. But once Jimmy took off to find his next fix, my boss did neither. Instead, he called Laura. I pretended to keep working as I listened to their conversation.

"That check you gave Jimmy is down here at the store.

Come by the house tonight, and I'll give it back. Otherwise, I'll cash it first thing in the morning."

I could hear her screams, though the actual words were undecipherable. Through her tirade, Doyle merely smiled and held the phone a few inches from his ear. When the racket subsided, he sighed and said, "Maybe next time you'll be smart enough not to hire one of my friends." Then he hung up.

I was full of questions...

"Are you crazy?"

"What if she really does hire someone else?"

"What if she shows up at your house with a gun?"

Clearly amused by my bubbling disbelief, Doyle answered in order.

"As a bed bug."

"She won't."

"And not if, but WHEN she shows up, I'll be the one with the loaded gun." Doyle grabbed his crotch and winked.

No doubt it was my gaping mouth which prompted Doyle to share a bit of his personal philosophy when it came to women.

"Laura doesn't really want to see me dead."

I couldn't help but laugh. "Funny since she's tried to kill you twice now. Ever hear the story about the third time being the charm?"

"Quit interrupting me, boy." He scolded me in the same manner and tone as Foghorn Leghorn did that little chicken hawk that was always trying to gnaw on his leg.

"If Laura really wanted to kill me, she wouldn't have revved her engine before she released the brake. Nor would she have hired a half-wit friend of mine to assassinate me."

"Only famous people get assassinated," I pointed out. "People like you get murdered. And do you really wanna put your trust in a crack head like Jimmy?"

Doyle narrowed his eyes. He studied me for a second. "You know what your biggest problem is?"

I shook my head. "Probably not, but my problems are nowhere near as big as yours."

"Nothing of yours is as big as mine," he said, "but genetics can't be helped."

When I didn't laugh he continued.

"Your biggest problem is you're predictable. Like the damn sun coming up in the east. Even worse, you think the entire frickin' world is just as predictable. That's why you're not getting any. Even high school girls crave excitement."

He was right, of course. In more ways than I cared to admit, but excitement and unpredictability aren't all they're cracked up to be. My attempts at flower theft were proof of that, but like any teenage boy in the throes of puberty, I didn't let that rocky start to my pursuit of the fairer sex derail me.

After Darlene and I parted ways, I went out a few times with a friend of hers named Christy. That had been over the summer. Christy was a nice enough girl, but a bit dingy. It's doubtful I ever would have dated her if she hadn't initiated things by calling me. Apparently Darlene had implied to her we would make a good couple.

Who knows? Maybe Christy had a thing for crumpled flowers and clumsy guys. But like I said, we only went out a time or two before I decided to move on.

Doyle, on the other hand, decided to move backward rather than forward. Laura did come to his house that night. He gave back her ill-intentioned check, and she gave him enough to erase the fact she'd tried to off him twice. They began dating again, and before spring break, they'd retied the knot. It didn't take a genius to see that knot was actually a noose, but I can't be too critical, I suppose, because after Christy, I too decided to revisit an old well.

Back in ninth grade I'd attended a party at a certain girl's house. Yes, Samantha Blake's. And at that party a good old game of spin-the-bottle broke out. A few rounds in and the bottle stopped dead on me. Oh, but did I get selected to kiss Samantha Blake? Of course not. The powers that be decreed I kiss Anna Ochoa, and kiss we did. With all the grace and romance of two embarrassed fifteen-year-olds. That had been my first ever kiss, and now two years later, I decided to ask Anna out on a date. After all, she hadn't gagged or run screaming from the room after that kiss. Our lips had touched. Surely that meant she would agree to simple date.

Or so you would think, but Anna said no. Looking like a slack-jawed idiot, I stood there in the hall outside of Mrs. Duckett's English classroom stunned. I'd been confident she would say yes. So much so that I didn't know what to say or do.

"Look, you're a nice guy and all, but my dad won't let me date white guys." And with that, Anna flounced away to join a gaggle of her giggling friends.

Once I recovered from the initial surprise, I took the rejection in stride. Things could have been worse. She could have said, "Hell no, I won't go on a date with you. Kissing you once was bad enough."

Later, during our senior year, Anna Ochoa became Mrs. Robbie Williams. That was about six months before she gave birth to a blue-eyed, blond little boy that looked exactly like his dad. Wonder what her father thought of that?

Doyle and Laura meanwhile, were divorced a second time before Labor Day rolled around, proving the past is a nice place to visit, but a mighty shitty place to live.

Chapter Six

The Big Pecker

At Pearl's the customer didn't always come to us. Sometimes, we went to them. From animal feed to flea collars. Pesticides to pepper plants. Big orders or small. We hauled our wares direct to the buyer, as long as they lived within fifteen or twenty miles of Amarillo. When I say we, I mostly mean me. I was also the feed store delivery boy.

Now there is a certain kind of movie, the kind that used to come in a blue box from rental stores, but these days is readily available on the internet or as a pay-per-view purchase. The kind of movie with the funky bom-chicka-bow-wow musical score, and really bad actors who have other, shall we say, assets. In those kinds of movies the unsuspecting delivery boy shows up, pizza box in hand, to find a bevy of blonde coeds, or a seductress of an older woman, or sometimes even a shy, timid lonely girl with a sudden urge to shed not only her inhibitions but also her clothes. Picture the guy standing there on the porch, totally unaware of the raucous experience awaiting him on the other side of the door. Now

I don't know about pizza delivery guys, but that kind of crap never happened to me.

Not even once.

Nary a single sex-starved redhead nor buxom brunette ever answered my knock. Apparently that kind of spontaneous horniness doesn't strike women upon the sight of a delivery boy with a fifty-pound bag of chicken scratch hoisted upon his shoulder. If it did, you can bet your rolled oats that Doyle, not me, would have made the deliveries.

That's not to say that I didn't encounter some mighty peculiar sights. Like chickens. In the house. Walking around the kitchen. In the middle of the city, no less. For those of you not overly familiar with the fowl, let me first say, chickens are nasty. They cannot be potty-trained, or if they can, none of our customers bothered teaching their cluckers. I'm not talking about one or two chickens. I'm talking about houses with fifteen or sixteen Rhode Island Reds running around inside. I recall one home where a woman let me in and directed me to put the sack of feed in the pantry. Sitting at the kitchen table, her husband was eating a bowl of who-knows-what, while not a foot away from the man's meal, a full grown rooster scratched and pecked at the crumbs on the wood surface. Call me crazy, but the only way I want a chicken on my table is after it's been rolled in flour and fried.

I also made the occasional delivery to Ginger, the woman with the strange infatuation for her pet goat, Wagner. As an artist, there were times when Ginger was too caught up in her latest painting to venture forth and hang out at the store debating politics with Doyle. When that was the case, I fetched Wagner's vittles. As if he was a child and not a goat, Wagner had his very own room, as well as the run of the house.

To Ginger's credit, I never spotted as much as a single goat hair on any of her furniture. Nor did I ever see or smell anything to make me believe Wagner did his business indoors. Ginger was a clean and otherwise normal lady with a strange and complex love for her pet goat.

Sadly that wasn't the case with all of our delivery customers. Most kept their pets and livestock outside where they belonged, but over time I encountered potbellied pigs, ferrets, twelve-foot-long snakes, llamas, miniature donkeys, horses, cows, hedgehogs, lizards, birds of all types, and of course tons of dogs and cats, all inside houses. Granted, the horse was a sick foal, the cow a miniature breed, and the llamas actually had an old house just to themselves.

Nevertheless, none of the critters I ever encountered compared to the wanton vixens visited by the pepperoni peddlers of movie fame. Nor were the animal infested houses my worst stop. That designation befell upon a place simply called, THE RANCH.

Every two weeks I headed north, five or six miles out of Amarillo, with three hundred pounds of horse feed, two hundred pounds of dog food, and several bags of ratite pellets. All in fifty-pound sacks. The guy who ordered the stuff was never home, so per his instructions, I'd park the truck at the gate, load two sacks at a time on my shoulder, and lug the load out into the pasture where an old boxcar served as a feed shed. Making six trips back and forth while toting that much feed was bad enough, but this particular field was a gauntlet of danger.

The wrought iron sign above the gate read THE RANCH, but in truth the exotic menagerie was more of a collection. Something akin to a redneck's personal zoo. There was a zebra, a couple of Sicilian donkeys, a herd of Nubian goats, several dozen chickens of varying breeds, a handful of miniature cows, two or three mangy looking hounds, a flock of guineas, a passel of peacocks, and one mean, nasty emu. All in the same enclosed area.

The whole four or five mesquite-filled acres were enclosed by an eight-foot high chain link fence. There was a drive-in gate, but it was always padlocked with a thick, rusty chain, so I was forced to use the small, walk-in entry. Considering I had to make many trips back and forth, with a hundred pounds of grain balanced on my shoulder, the fifty yards separating said gate from the shed made the task hard enough. Add in the fact I had to dodge crap piles as varied in size as the assortment of animals that left them, all-the-while finagling my way past low-hanging, thorn-covered mesquite branches, and the job was downright miserable. And come summertime, the Texas heat created rivulets of eye-stinging sweat. But none of those hazards compared to the sneaky, back-door attacks of a nearly seven-foot-tall bird.

Emus are the second largest bird by height, ranking behind their ratite cousin, the ostrich, and this particular one came running every time I pulled up. Not to offer its feathered greetings, but rather with the hope of pecking my eyes out. I hated making that delivery, but one hot August afternoon that was exactly the chore facing me.

It was one of those days where not a single cloud decorated the sky, and the mere idea of a breeze seemed as distant as the Serengeti. Parking the truck in the bar ditch near the gate, I stepped out into the knee-high weeds, knowing the laces of my work boots would be full of sand burrs by the time I finished carrying the feed inside. Strands of rusted baling wire held the gate shut. Untwisting them, I eyed the collection of animals on the other side. The chickens and guineas had flocked to the gate as usual, but I didn't care about them. The bird I worried about was much bigger. To my surprise, the emu was nowhere to be seen. My last trip to the place had ended with nasty whelp on the back of my neck, and I aimed to avoid another such injury. Matter of fact, I'd sworn never to venture back, but both Doyle and the owner of the bird had convinced me the emu was easily handled.

"Englebert is harmless enough," the man explained. "Ya just gotta maintain eye contact with 'im. It's a game for

Englebert. First time he thinks you ain't lookin', he'll run in and git ya."

Maintaining eye contact seemed an easy enough solution back at the store, but now with the chore at hand I didn't feel nearly as confident. The Sicilian donkeys were a bit cantankerous as well, but a few angry shouts tended to keep them at bay. When it was hot, the donkeys hung out in the shade cast off by the boxcar, and they didn't like being forced to move simply so I could open the door. If I got anywhere close to either ass's ass it would kick. More than one dent in the side of the boxcar testified to their power, but I'm proud to say they'd never managed to get a hoof on me.

Hot as it was, I guessed the emu had joined the donkeys in the shade of the feed shed. Probably the zebra too. Loading the first two sacks of grain onto my left shoulder, I eased through the gate. Off to my right sat a large metal stock tank full of green, algae-filled water. Already sweat had begun to seep from my pores, so despite the slime growing in the stock tank, the water looked inviting. Sometimes I dipped my hat under the inlet pipe, but today there wasn't enough air moving to pump in fresh water.

Halfway to my destination, the emu stepped out into the dusty path. Like two gunfighters in the streets of an old cowtown, we sized one another up.

Perspiration trickled down my neck. The one hundred pounds of feed weighed heavy on my shoulder. I took a step.

So did the bird.

I took another.

Englebert sidled off the path.

"Oh no you don't," I said, turning to match the angle of the bird. I inched forward.

Englebert matched my every movement by creeping slightly forward and to the left.

It took a good bit longer than normal, but I eventually made the safety of the boxcar by walking in slow pirouettes. No doubt I looked like a fool slow-dancing with an emu, but I was willing to do the tango if that's what it took to avoid being pecked by the beast. Back and forth I went, continuing to do the redneck ballet every step of the way. I made four or five trips without incident. The pesky bird orbited around me, but made no mad rushes.

Then, the animals ganged up on me.

Backing into the boxcar, I sat the sacks down, relieved that I'd safely made another trip. One more load and I would be finished, but the combination of the heat and the extra effort of walking in circles had left me winded, so I leaned against the metal door jam to catch my breath.

The sheet metal popped from the weight of my body. The noise startled a barn cat. The cat barreled out from behind the sacks. The fleeing cat scared the shitake mushrooms out of me. My yelled expletives, combined with the cat dashing out of the shed and running between the asses' legs, incited the donkeys who brayed at the top of their lungs. The zebra chimed in with its odd, laugh-like bleats.

Distracted by the crazy donkey, I didn't notice Englebert creeping up in the shadow of the boxcar... until the oversized drumstick dashed in and pecked me right in the back of the head. Stunned by the blow, I staggered back and fell butt first into the box car. An angry knot formed on my head almost instantly, as did my fury. Grabbing an empty fivegallon bucket, I flung the plastic container at Englebert. Missing my target, I next hurled a pair of linesman's pliers.

You'd be surprised how agile emus are when playing dodgeball.

Two rolls of baling wire, several more hand tools, and a Folgers can full of nuts and bolts followed, but not a damn thing I flung at the gangly bird found its mark. And worse yet, picking the customer's stuff up off the ground made it impossible to maintain eye contact. Before all was said and done, Englebert pecked me half a dozen times that day. Had I caught the damned bird, I would've skinned the thing and made me a new pair of boots. Maybe even a wallet to match. Instead, I got a body full of nasty bruises and purple welts. Still seething, even after the drive back to town, I stomped inside Pearl's and relayed my sad tale to Doyle.

He listened while I ranted about the barn cat scaring the donkey, and about Englebert dashing in to peck me while I was distracted. I told him about me getting mad and throwing everything I could at the giant bird, only to make it easy to get attacked over and over again. I wrapped up my angry little tale, expecting to hear some sort of sympathetic statement from my boss.

Instead Doyle looked at me, grinned, and said, "I've been trying to tell you. Let a little pussy scare your ass, and a big pecker is bound to get you in the end."

Doyle's punchline about my pain might seem homophobic in today's time, but it wasn't gay people he feared so much as it was fear itself. Back then I marveled how nothing seemed to scare my boss, but in hindsight I believe Doyle had his anxieties just like everyone else in the world. I can't help but wonder how that realization would have changed the way I saw my boss. Would I have so eagerly followed his example had I know his brazen behavior was not an act of genuine bravado, but a coping mechanism? Would I have developed the confidence to take a few chances of my own? Would I have prevented myself all the trouble that followed?

Maybe, but then again the boredom just might have killed me.

Chapter Seven

Menudo and Mormons

Doyle's brand of wisdom trended towards the crude. Despite, or maybe because of my boss's crass nature, his philosophies and advice clamped onto me like a tick on a stray mutt. Usually painful, often bloodletting, and always educational in a warped kind of way, Doyle's example provided the beacon for my journey into manhood.

Until my junior year of high school, I traveled a rather straight and narrow highway. But early on in that junior year I decided to hell with pavement, street lamps, and ready-made routes to success. I wanted adventure, thrilling scenery, and mysterious trails through the undergrowth of life.

As a young kid, my friends were determined by who lived within walking or biking distance. That restriction fell to the wayside once I got my driver's license. The ability to drive didn't cause me to suddenly dislike all my old buddies from elementary and junior high. Those guys were still my friends, but a ride of my own meant I could venture farther and hang out with people I shared more in common with than a neighborhood.

One such person was a kid named Cody Hawkins. Cody was eighteen, a senior, one year ahead of me when we started hanging out. Like most things that happen to teenage boys, a girl was to blame for my friendship with Cody. Sherry was her name. She was my age, and we'd gone to school together since the seventh grade. Truth be told, I didn't know her all that well, but Cody seemed to think I did, and for whatever reason he decided I was his best shot to get close. Despite my dubious matchmaking credentials they did wind up dating for a short time. Less than a month as I recall. That was all it took for Sherry to realize Cody was a complete and total jackass.

Sadly, it took me much longer to discern that fact. In the end, I became good friends with Sherry and I'm proud to say we've now maintained that relationship for more than two decades. But Cody was a different story.

Cody was a wannabe bull rider. To be fair, he was a bull rider, just not a very good one. In the five or six months we palled around, never did I witness him make a full eight-second ride. Not even once.

Once upon a time my dad had been a rodeo man—a steer wrestler, as well as a calf roper. But my dad never was around long enough to teach me any of those skills, and I sure hadn't inherited any. So while I considered myself something of a cowboy, I didn't actually possess any credentials for the title. Guess that made me the wannabe in this equation, and maybe it explains why I was drawn to Cody. As if being his friend would turn me into what I thought I wanted to be.

Cody did introduce me to a lot of so-called cowboy stuff: the music of Chris LeDoux, Copenhagen, and of course, cold cans of Coors Light. The Copenhagen was a short-lived encounter. I bought one can, dipped less than half of it, and decided rancid breath and black shit stuck between my teeth really wasn't the image I wanted to portray. I've moved on to better beer than Coors Light, but my appreciation for a cold brewski and a good ballad has far outlasted my friendship with Cody Hawkins.

Our days of being buddies ended the night Cody drank a bottle of Jaegermeister and then decided to peg me upside the head with a cue ball. The throbbing ugly red welt above my right temple dramatically increased my ability to see Cody in the same light as Sherry.

Booze, tunes, and a dislike for billiards. I can thank Cody for those things, but his impact went beyond that. He also brought me into the fold of a group of friends. A group I never would've been a part of otherwise. A group that brought me pain, pleasure, and my first tactile taste of adulterated fun.

Working for Doyle at Pearl's Feed and Seed, I'd been exposed to my share of carnal pleasure. But exposure and firsthand experience are as different as riding a wild stallion from those ponies chained in a circle at the petting zoo. Funny thing is, only now in the telling of this story do I realize just how closely my misadventures away from the Pearl's mirrored those I bore witness to at work.

Feed sacks are not created equal. Take range cubes for example. A fifty-pound sack came in a bag slightly longer and more narrow than most of the others. Its contents hard and lumpy, a stack of range cube bags made for a poor bed. Conversely, steam-rolled oats came in large, wide bags. And the oats themselves were soft and pliable. Therefore, a stack of rolled oats made a mighty fine makeshift bed. Stacked side by side, in groups of four, they formed a raised platform not unlike an extra firm mattress. Or so I assumed, given Doyle's regular use of the rolled oats.

Remember Tasha? The newlywed with the shoulders of an NFL linebacker and the face of Doyle's dog Snuggles? She was a member of the odd assortment of regulars that hung out at Pearl's. Tasha was a woman with lots of problems. She had a husband she couldn't stand, despite the fact they'd been married less than a year. She owned two horses she couldn't really afford to feed. And as previously mentioned, Tasha possessed a disposition that by comparison made her bull-doggish face seem downright luscious.

Never one to ignore a damsel in distress, Doyle was quick to aid Tasha with her first two problems. Sadly, not even a virile guy like Doyle contained enough machismo to permanently transfigure her surly temperament. Oh, but he could make her happy in the short term. You see, Doyle and Tasha had an arrangement. She didn't have to pay for her horse feed, long as she came in every so often to test the comfort and durability of the rolled oats. I was never privy to the finer details of their arrangement. I do not know if two-hundred pounds of sweet grain equaled one visit to the oat pallet, or if five bags of horse feed and two bales of alfalfa were equal to a roll in the hay. But I do know that both parties were quite pleased with their little business deal. It's worth mentioning, not one cent came out of Doyle's pocket since his dad actually owned the store and ultimately paid for the bartered horse feed.

I must, however, confess. Doyle and Tasha were not the only ones to gain pleasure from their feed room trysts. I too enjoyed a few benefits from their illicit arrangement. Before you get the wrong idea, let me say I didn't enjoy THOSE kind of benefits. Nothing so perverse. No, my satisfaction was not of libidinal roots, but of a vengeful, mischievous nature.

Doyle never let a chance to harangue, harass, or humiliate me slip by, and after having worked for him better than a year, I was equally opportunistic, though at times a tad slow to recognize the potential of a particular situation. As was the case with Tasha and Doyle's feed room rendezvous.

Tasha would show up, always in the late afternoon, reeking of cheap perfume that smelled more like the sweet floral aroma of a funeral parlor than it did a fancy French whore. Then again, French whores do not peddle their wares in feed stores.

Silhouetted in the doorway, Tasha would stand with one hand on her hip until Doyle made eye-contact. At which point, he would turn to me and say, "That last bag of sweet grain Tasha bought was all dried out. I'm gonna take her in the back and make certain we find one that's good and moist. Stay up front and use the intercom if you need anything."

For those of you who've never raised animals, I should explain that sweet grain can, and does, dry out due to the fact the grains are mixed together with molasses, thus the name.

Some might assume, as perhaps Tasha did, that Doyle concocted the stale grain story as a gallant way to protect her reputation. To that idea I cry, Bullshit! If Doyle cared one iota about Tasha's image, he would've met her away from the store. Tasha was not Doyle's only mid-day dance partner, she just happened to be the only one he did the watusi with right there at the store. My boss didn't speak out to protect Tasha, but rather to remind me about the intercom. Actually "intercom" is the wrong word, what served as communication between the feed room and the register area was little more than a glorified baby monitor.

The person or persons in the feed room could only hear those up front if they wanted to be heard and pressed the talk button. Whereas, any- and everyone at the register could hear EVERYTHING that went on in the back—simply by turning up the volume.

Stunned at the time, I listened to Doyle and Tasha's first tryst long enough to verify they were doing what I'd imagined. Then I turned the volume down as low as it would go. Don't get me wrong, I wasn't the least bit surprised Doyle was willing to screw back in the feed room.

I'd worked for him long enough that his lustful thoughts or actions no longer carried shock value. But I was amazed that a woman, any woman, was willing to shed her clothes and fornicate among the dust, spider webs, and earthy scents of mice and grain. Then again, maybe that "earthy" aura was exactly what Tasha enjoyed. Actually, thanks to the intercom, I learned all too well what Tasha liked.

Weekday afternoons tended to be slow around the store, so for a while Doyle and Tasha got lucky, in more ways than one, and managed to complete their transaction without interruption. But then came the day Mrs. Esparza arrived for her weekly bag of hen scratch. Luckily the elderly woman was hard of hearing, otherwise she would've heard Doyle's string of angry expletives when I turned on the intercom and announced the need for a fifty-pound sack of chicken scratch.

Getting disrupted in the throes of satisfaction was bad enough. To be derailed for the sake of a four-dollar-and-twenty-five-cent bag of chicken feed, the cheapest sack of grain we sold, made it especially hard to take. Speaking of hard, it was the sight of Doyle, awkwardly bent forward, trying desperately to carry said sack of hen scratch while concealing his swollen appreciation for Tasha that made me first realize the unmined vein of gold at hand.

Mrs. Esparza also took notice of Doyle's painful posture, though she misread its cause. "You should not carry heavy things when you have a bad back," she said. "Let the boy do such things." She pointed at me.

Like most hard-of-hearing folks, Mrs. Esparza talked way too loud, so her voice carried well enough for me to hear through the open door. I could not, however, make out Doyle's reply as he dumped his load into the trunk. By load I, of course, mean the sack of grain.

Mrs. Esparza shook her head. "You do not look fine to me. You still do not stand up straight, like normal."

Doyle turned still hunched over. Eager to escape, he tried to get away, but Mrs. Esparza wasn't finished. "I'll make you a batch of menudo tonight and bring for your lunch tomorrow. Menudo is good for you. Will help build strong muscles and bones!"

Of course, Mrs. Esparza had no idea that it was actually a single muscle, plaguing Doyle. Therefore, she brought in a huge Tupperware bowl of menudo the very next morning. Doyle slurped away while Mrs. Esparza proudly smiled. He offered me some, but tripe soup grossed me out more than the top layer of rolled oats sacks. I refused to handle those sacks after Doyle and Tasha began using them as their mattress. The word printed before oats was "rolled" not "soiled," and for three twenty-five an hour I wasn't too eager to discover which bags fell into what category.

After Mrs. Esparza's visit, I made certain Doyle and Tasha never enjoyed another peaceful encounter. I'd listen and wait until they were thoroughly engaged, then I'd claim to need a hundred pounds of rabbit pellets, or half a ton of range cubes, or I'd call one of my buddies and tell them to call right back.

At which point, I'd announce over the intercom that Doyle had an important phone call.

Sometimes he believed me, other times not, but his doubt was tempered by the fact that on more than one occasion, there actually was a customer in need of something. It became a game between Doyle and me, a game for which Tasha rightfully blamed me for ruining her fun. She glared through narrowed eyes anytime I was in the same room. I'll confess her withering stares made the hair on the back of my neck stand on end, but on the bright side, Tasha had stopped speaking to me, so I was spared hearing her grating, nasal-tinged voice.

She even went so far as to beg Doyle to fire me, but deep down he enjoyed the game. It added a degree of excitement to the package. A goal to achieve. Could he tell by my voice if I was lying? Could he finish before I got bored enough to harass them? Could he make a mad dash out to load several hundred pounds of grain and maintain his erection without the customer thinking he was overly excited to see them? Tasha came for the sex, but Doyle was in it for the sport. And he usually took home the gold, but on one occasion I truly got the better of him.

Doyle learned quickly to look outside when I used the intercom. If he didn't spot a vehicle parked out front, he quickly called bullshit to my interruption and carried on with his business. Knowing he would never spot their bicycles, I took great pleasure when two Mormon missionaries pedaled up and leaned their bikes against the front of the store.

Religion was one of Doyle's favorite subjects. He loved to quote the Bible and argue various doctrines. These two particular guys had been in the store only a week before, and my boss had engaged them in quite the lengthy conversation. As promised, they had returned with more pamphlets to support their beliefs.

Before the guys stepped inside, I pressed the talk button. "Doyle, there are a couple of guys here to see you."

"Did you hear a car?" I heard him ask Tasha. "I didn't hear a car," he said before she could respond.

I pushed the button again. "I'm telling you there are two guys here to see you."

"Quit jack-assing around, Travis. I'm not in the mood to play your fucking games today."

By now the two missionaries had entered the store. Both bore puzzled expressions as I pushed the button yet again. "So, what? You want me to tell them to come back another time?"

"Go fuck yourself." This time Tasha's twang filled the air. "Can't you turn that thing off while I'm here? It creeps me out he can hear us. When are you going to fire that pervert?"

"Don't worry about him," Doyle said. "Just focus right here on my eyes. Look at me. Yeah, just like that. How does that feel?"

"Uhhh," Tasha let out a long, moaning sigh.

I pushed the button yet again, so Tasha and Doyle could hear me. Although this time I addressed the now blushing bicyclists. "Sorry guys, but Doyle is otherwise engaged at the moment. Maybe you should come back later."

The taller of the two simply nodded and backed toward the door, but the other young man said, "We will pray for him."

I released the talk button in time to hear Doyle say, "Shit, there really was somebody up there."

Doyle managed to get his pants zipped and his butt up front in time to see the two guys pedal away on their bicycles. Shaking his head, he stared at their retreating backs. "Shit. I thought you were jacking around with me again. Why didn't you tell me it was those Mormon guys on bikes? I might've believed you."

Nodding I said, "Yeah, maybe, but this way was a lot more fun."

Between what I detected as genuine embarrassment for sinning so blatantly in front of such devout religious men, and irritation for letting me get the better of him, Doyle, for the first time ever, refused to go back and finish the job. Tasha left in a tizzy and vowed never to return. That proclamation lasted only until the next time she and her horses required sustenance.

Of course, her hatred for me only grew from that day forward. I wish I could say my triumph was a lasting victory, but alas, I cannot. Because soon after ruining Tasha's fun, I discovered firsthand just how cruel karma can be.

Chapter Eight

Feeding the Chickens

Your reap what you sow.
What goes around comes around.
A taste of your own medicine.

There are a million clichés that assert the exact same principal—Karma. Of course, no one I knew called it "karma" when I was growing up. The very word was too new age-esque for either my family, or the clientele at Pearl's Feed and Seed.

Even now, twenty years later, most Bible-belters want to dismiss the phenomenon as Hindu and Buddhist mumbo-jumbo, despite the familiar biblical refrain of "Do unto others." I'd heard that scripture as a small child in Sunday School, but only after I ruined Doyle and Tasha's fun, and experienced Karma's sting firsthand, did I become a true believer.

The Baillouxs were central to that group of friends Cody Hawkins had introduced me to. When I say introduced, I do not actually mean introduce as in first met.

I'd been classmates with two of the three Baillouxs since my first year of high school. Therefore, I knew who they were. I'd even heard about the parties at their house. So I was eager and excited when Cody told me they were having a get-together on Friday. He gave me directions to their place out east of town and told me to bring at least a twelve pack of beer.

That Friday I handed Doyle twenty bucks, nearly a full day's pay for me, and asked if he'd run down to the liquor store and buy me a case of Coors Light. If a twelve pack was good, I figured a case would be even better.

Agreeing, Doyle took the cash, saying only, "You oughta at least ask me to buy you some good beer."

That evening, I headed out to the Bailloux place thirsty for adventure and excitement. John was the eldest of the three Bailloux siblings. Nearly twenty, he should have graduated two years earlier. I'd be grossly underestimating the truth if I described John as merely challenged when it came to pursuits within the classroom, but to his credit, he'd hung in there and finally reached his final year of high school. Heavily adorned with freckles, John's skin was the color of a tarnished penny. Tall and thin, he was freakishly strong and devoutly loyal to those he considered a friend. Those he called something else definitely did not want to get on John's bad side. Especially after he'd been drinking. For a high school kid, even one several years past his original expiration date, John could down vast quantities of beer. The case I brought my first invite would not have carried John beyond a festive Friday night.

Candy Bailloux was two years younger than her brother, but she did not share John's intellectual inabilities. Therefore, they both happened to be seniors in the same graduating class. Candy also had lots of freckles, but she wore them better than her brother. Given her curvaceous body, Candy wore any- and everything well. Most especially, the tight Rocky Mountain jeans she and all the so-called cowgirls wore back in those days. Candy didn't have the kind of face that made fellas instantly fall in love. Truth be told, few if any would've described her as pretty at first sight. But Candy possessed an allure that snuck up on a guy. A detached, uncaring attitude that came off sexy enough to seduce most every boy in our FFA class. Funny thing was, Candy turned down every guy who asked her out.

Not to be deterred, most of the guys settled for hanging out at the Bailloux homestead on Friday and Saturday nights. I'd heard plenty of tales and rumors about the Bailloux soirees but, being a year behind them in school, I'd never been invited. That changed when Cody Hawkins brought me into the fold.

The three Bailloux teenagers, John, Candy, and Missy, lived with their mom and stepfather in a ramshackle house several miles east of Amarillo's city limits. A junkyard bordered one side of their place, but it was hard to tell where the exact property line ended, since the Bailloux homestead also housed dozens of broken down and rusted automobiles.

I first visited in late September, when it was still warm

outside. The family's herd of goats and chickens chased grasshoppers through the maze of battered and abused vehicles, while we teenagers perched on the hoods and drank beer. I can't say for certain whether the Bailloux's mom and step-dad condoned or even knew what we were doing, but my guess is they simply didn't care long as we left them alone. Once fall and winter chased us inside, I discovered the adults spent their evenings sitting around a scarred Formica table. Rum, whiskey, and vodka bottles littered the surface and a cloud of cigarette smoke hovered above their heads.

John and Candy smoked as well, however their little sister, Missy, did not. Nor did she drink. Only a freshman, Missy had also managed to avoid the freckles that so prominently decorated her siblings. Oh, she had a few dotting her nose and cheekbones, but her skin wasn't completely covered like the others. Unfortunately, Missy also lacked Candy's curves. But Missy did possess one thing her older sister did not—a healthy infatuation for yours truly. I, of course, missed that set of clues. I had no idea Missy was smitten with me. At least not until it was too late.

Most nights there were ten to fifteen of us gathered around drinking. We swapped stories. Lied about things we claimed to have done. Bragged about stuff we were going to do. And of course, hoped we'd get invited to help feed the chickens.

Before even my first visit, Cody mentioned the chickens.

At first all he'd say was, "If Candy asks you to help feed the chickens, make damn sure you go."

I pestered him for details, until he finally relented and said, "Candy gives the best blowjobs."

Now to a high school boy, the words blow and job used in direct sequence with one another are mystical in nature. The very idea of being on the receiving end of such an act is enough to stimulate the body and mind of any pubescent male. Part fantasy and part legend, blowjobs were the sexual equivalent of Sasquatch. Every teenage boy had heard stories of their existence, yet most of us had no firsthand knowledge.

So imagine my gape-mouthed expression the first time Candy Bailloux finished off a beer, stood, and said, "I better go feed the chickens." Her eyes roamed the circle of anxious looking boys until they settled upon a senior named Steve Golds. "Steve, you wanna help me?"

A half hour later Steve returned to the group, looking happier than a tabloid editor with photographic proof that not only was Elvis still alive, but also shacked up in a love nest with Princess Di.

I knew then and there that Cody's stories were true. Over the coming months, Steve got the nod more than once. As did Cody. A handful of other guys made single visits, but not once did Candy's gaze linger upon me. Oh, Candy talked to me and made eye-contact with me, but never when she searched for her next partner to help feed the chickens.

Rejection, even rejection by omission, is not something teenage boys handle well. I was no exception. I enjoyed John's company as well as the camaraderie of being part of a large group of friends. And I suppose sitting around drinking beer with a bunch of seniors made me feel older and somehow more grown up, but I'd be lying if I didn't admit I longed for the chance to help feed the chickens. At least once.

I thought I'd get my chance when Cody got drunk and beaned me upside the head with that cue ball. Actually, when that first happened I assumed my days of being invited to the Bailloux's were over. After all, Cody was the one who invited me to their house. But when I didn't show up that Friday, John swung by Pearl's Saturday afternoon and asked why.

Stuffing a wad of Copenhagen between his lip and gum, John listened to my explanation. "Yeah, he was bragging about it last night. But fuck Cody. He's a prick anyway."

"Yeah, I know, but I don't wanna cause any trouble out at your house." Continuing to stack the seventy-pound salt blocks we'd gotten in earlier that day, I said, "I owe him an ass-kicking, and after a few beers it would be damned hard not to collect."

"He shows up, and I'll smack the fucker for you," John said. "I already told him not to come back. Candy is the only one who might care, but she can find someone else to blow."

I stopped stacking the heavy blocks and looked at John. The fact he knew what Candy did with her helpers in their feed shed shouldn't have surprised me. Her "giving-nature" was no secret amongst our circle, but John was her brother, and tough as he was, I doubted any of the guys boasted to him about their hummers.

"Besides that," John said, "You're twice that shithead's size. He wouldn't have the balls to stop with your truck there."

That night, Candy showed more interest in me than she ever had. Sitting side-by-side on the Bailloux's couch, I showed her the exact spot where the flying cue ball had struck my head.

Gingerly touching the area just above my temple, she said, "I can still feel the knot. You should've kicked his ass."

"Yeah, but I wasn't exactly thinking clearly. By the time I figured out what the hell was going on, Brad had thrown me out."

Brad was a forty-something-year-old dude that owned a teen bar. A place where kids hung out shooting pool, dancing, and sneaking liquor into their cans of soda when they thought no one was looking. Cody had smuggled a bottle of Jagermeister inside his boot that night. He kept refilling his soda can with the Jager, and somewhere in the course of emptying the bottle, decided I was pissing him off.

We'd been shooting pool for several hours when he reared back and flung the cue ball straight at my head. While I lay on the ground, he convinced Brad and his bouncers that

I'd been picking on him. As John later pointed out, I was nearly twice Cody's size, so they had little trouble believing his version of the story.

But none of that seemed important when Candy's fingers were touching my skin. She was so close I could feel her warm breath on my ear. The hairs on the back of my neck stood on end, and they were not alone. Candy had already finished off several beers so I knew it was getting close to time for her to go feed the chickens. Surely tonight would be my lucky night.

Or so I thought. But before I could get too cocky, Missy walked up and said, "I already fed the chickens, so you wouldn't have to."

Normally Missy hung out on the periphery of our group. She was always somewhere around, but never involved in the conversation. While we sat around drinking and talking, she sat at a distance, often with a book open. Sometimes I'd ask her what she was reading, and if I was familiar with the novel we'd discuss it, but more times than not she held some Harlequin Romance I knew nothing about. Delivering the news about the chickens having already been fed, she stared hard at her sister for several long seconds before walking away.

Chickens use their beaks to pick out and separate the smallest bit of grain from the dirt and sand. Right about then my own pecker's opportunity was about to be lost in a ginormous dune of bad timing.

"How many chickens do y'all have?" I asked. "I'd like to see them sometime."

Steve Golds laughed. "I bet you would."

At that, almost everyone laughed. Even John and Candy, but Missy was not so amused. Instead of laughing, she stared at her older sister with a look of pure hatred.

Candy didn't seem to notice, but when the laughter died, she no longer seemed to notice me either. Instead, she looked over at John and said, "Toss me another beer. I didn't feel like feeding the damn chickens anyway."

The months slipped by and not once did Candy even hint I might be the one to help feed the chickens. Matter of fact, it became rare for anyone to be offered that opportunity. As her graduation neared, Candy's primary focus settled upon leaving Texas. Her lone goal was to pack up and move to Florida. Candy worked part-time for a veterinarian and she confessed she'd been saving her paychecks for years. In April, she showed us a one-way plane ticket to Miami. Her flight left the day after graduation.

John, on the other hand, had been saving for a pickup and by mid-May he had enough for the down payment on a Chevy 454 SS. After a few beers, talk turned to fast engines.

Steve had a beat-up old Mustang which he thought was the fastest thing on four wheels. There was a stretch of blacktop that led to the Bailloux's place, and long ago someone had painted two white stripes a quarter-mile apart. Many times a challenge had been tossed out among the crowd, only to be settled on that stretch of flat pavement. More times than not, Steve's Mustang won those challenges.

John knew cars and knew his heavy truck couldn't accelerate nearly as fast as Steve's Mustang, so he challenged him to a longer race. They haggled over the details of their wager and finally settled on a twelve pack. They were to race from the stop sign at the end of the road, all the way down to the narrow dirt cutoff that led to the Bailloux's front door. A distance of nearly a mile.

John and Steve got in their vehicles and drove off to the starting point, whereas the rest of the group walked down the dirt road toward what would be the finish line.

Cars never had been my thing, so I lingered, letting the rest of the group go on without me. When they'd all disappeared from sight, I grabbed a Coors Light from the cooler and leaned against the front fender of a battered old El Camino.

"Don't you wanna see who wins?"

I looked to the left, but didn't see Candy, though I knew by her voice she'd been the one to ask the question.

"Not really. It won't matter anyway. Whoever loses will want a rematch, and even if they lose a second time, they'll blame it on bad gas or a sticky carburetor or something." I popped open the beer and took a swig just as Candy sat up from where she'd been lying in the back of the El Camino's bed.

"You wanna help me feed the chickens then?"

Just like that, my chance was before me. I wouldn't get another as Candy was soon leaving. Leaving for good, she claimed.

I swallowed a mouthful of the suddenly warm beer and said, "Sure. Why not?"

My heart pounded when Candy hopped out of the car and headed back to the Bailloux's feed shed. My mind raced as I followed.

Sure, I'd been fantasizing about this very moment for months, but now that it was actually happening, I couldn't help but think of everything that could go wrong once we entered that feed shed.

Candy could expect me to make the first move.

Even if she made the first, second, and third move I still might screw it up. One dude at our school had forever been labeled as Quick Draw McGraw for being a bit too eager when his date merely touched him. Since we were surrounded by chickens, I had no doubt the school would be calling me Foghorn Leghorn were I to crow prematurely. The door no more than shut behind me when Candy turned and kissed me. I tried not to think about the places those lips had been as her hand found my zipper.

Now I suppose I could elaborately describe the thoughts and feelings of everything that happened after Candy reached for me. If I tried hard enough, I might even be able to extract a fancy metaphor out of the situation. But my memory is a bit clouded when it comes to recalling the finer details. I blame that on the lack of blood flow to my brain at that given time.

Knowing the inclination of teenage boys to lie and exaggerate, I'd always had my doubts to the authenticity of the claims about Candy and her skills. There in that feed shed, with the dirt floor and spider-web covered rafters, I fast became a true believer. At that given moment I would have believed most anything, so had Bigfoot walked in with a baby unicorn cradled in his hairy arms, I would've merely smiled and said, "The world is a wonderful place."

But it wasn't Bigfoot that walked in ... but rather, Missy Bailloux.

Missy stood there in the door frame for only a heartbeat before screeching, "I knew you were a slut! But did you have to be a bitchface, liar too?" She slammed the door and left. Dust filtered down from the ceiling.

Sighing, Candy rose to her feet. "She has a crush on you and I told her I wouldn't mess around with you."

I didn't know how to respond. Of course the awkwardness level was raised up a notch, or ten, by the fact my pants were still around my ankles.

Candy pointed to the door. "You should go talk to her."

"Me? What ... I ... uh ... What am I supposed to say?"

"It doesn't fucking matter what you say." Candy shook her head. "That's what none of you understand. We don't give a shit what you say as long as you say something. Why do y'all have to be so stupid?"

I wasn't sure exactly who the *y'all* and *they* included, but I did know that standing there, exposed, while Candy berated me, wasn't the ending I'd been hoping for. Yeah, I felt sort of guilty, but then again Candy had asked me to help feed the chickens. It's not like I'd dragged her back there against her will.

Zipping my pants, I said, "Look, I had no idea Missy liked me."

"Of course you didn't. Because you're blind and stupid. But now you know. So go talk to her."

"And tell her what?"

"That you like her, and you're sorry."

"Missy is nice and all, but I've never really thought about her like that."

Candy glared at me. "Don't be a dick."

"Me? I'm not the one that lied to my sister and made a promise I couldn't keep."

"Fuck you. Fuck all of you. I don't need any of this. I'll be gone in two weeks anyway." And with that, Candy left me alone in the feed shed.

Sitting on an old refrigerator that had been laid on its back and now served as a feed bin, I tried to figure out how the hell things had gone to shit so quickly. Not ten minutes ago, I'd been drinking a beer and having a good time hanging with friends. Now I had not one, but two, girls pissed off, a hard-on that refused to go away, and worse yet, I had to go back outside and face my hoard of drunken friends.

Karma must have been smiling at my dilemma. No doubt

she was high-fiving her sister Lady Luck as I exited that feed shed. On the surface, two Mormon dudes on bicycles and little sisters with crushes have little in common, but when you toss in Karma and her tit-for-tat brand of justice, the lesson can come from any angle.

What goes around, comes around.

Metaphorically speaking that is, because if Karma is involved then sometimes *What goes around* ... well, doesn't.

Chapter Nine

The Bantam Badass

My junior year of high school came to an end, and the onset of summer meant more hours at the feed store. Hours sweating and stacking sacks in the feed room alongside my coworker Jerry Greer, who was far from being a loyal pupil in the shower-a-day school of hygiene.

After a year and a half at Pearl's, Jerry didn't like my presence any more than he had the day I started. I would say he didn't like me any more than he ever had, but in truth, Jerry never bothered to try and get to know me. A cross between Barney Fife and Napoleon, Jerry took his job seriously. Certainly more seriously than our boss, even though Doyle had a more vested stake. To Jerry's way of thinking, the garden seeds and animal grain we sold fed the world. The pesticides rid the planet of evil, and the fertilizers gave life where there would otherwise be none. That summer Jerry decided the time had come to transform me into a model employee, molded in his own image. An employee who fully appreciated our role in making the universe a better place.

Doyle stroked Jerry's ego by allowing, even encouraging him to "keep me straight," though Doyle's motivation stemmed more from amusing himself than from a desire to keep Jerry happy, or to shape me into Jerry's image. The boss enjoyed our bickering, even instigated it. In one breath he'd say, "That's right, you tell him, Jerry. You gotta show these young kids how to do everything. They got no work ethic." Not two minutes later, Doyle would say to me, "Don't let him boss you around. Stand up. Be a man. Tell him to kiss your ass."

As time went on, I grew sick of trying to appease Jerry. By the start of my second summer at the store, I'd had a belly full of his anal tendencies, so I went out of my way to pluck at his nerves. Instead of starting each stack of feed with two sacks perpendicular to the wall like he preferred, I laid them out parallel. Jerry watered the plants first and the animals second. I reversed the order just to watch him shake his head.

I swept the floor differently. I counted change differently. And the thing that really pissed Jerry off—I answered the phone informally.

Copying Doyle's laid-back style, I greeted callers with a simple, "Feed store, can I help you?" whereas as Jerry opted for the more rigid, and poetic, "Pearl's Feed and Seed, we have whatever you need," which was exactly how Pearl had taught him back when she ran the joint.

Jerry's loyalty to the feed store's namesake did not end with the telephone greeting. At least once a month he tidied up the back corner of the store, the area that once housed Pearl's dress shop. Jerry would dust and clean off the files of dress patterns. He vacuumed the bolts of fabric and shined the mirrors in the dressing rooms, as if the woman who'd hired him was going to return one day soon and begin fitting brides and prom queens all over again. And once he started that project, there was no derailing him, regardless of how many customers needed help.

    I don't think Jerry necessarily liked Doyle any more than he did me, but as Pearl's offspring and the man in charge, I suppose Jerry felt duty-bound to at least try and hide his distaste for the boss.

    Doyle admitted on more than one occasion he would have run Jerry off long ago if the squirrelly little dude wasn't so damn fun to harass. Part of me wonders if Doyle didn't keep Jerry round just to see how much abuse a man could take. That summer, we found the answer.

    Both me and Doyle were right around six-foot-five. Jerry was at least a foot shorter. Matter of fact, he pretty much looked eye-to-eye with Austin, despite the fact Doyle's oldest had only just turned twelve. At least once a month Doyle made the two of them stand back-to-back and compare heights just to piss Jerry off.

    Even with about ten pounds of black wavy mop on top of his head, Jerry couldn't have tipped the scales much past a buck twenty-five, though according to his stories there were few men alive he hadn't whipped in a fight. He'd scaled mountain peaks, swam ocean channels, and bedded beauties on six of the seven continents. More than once Doyle asked him why he hadn't just fucked a seal or penguin simply to put a check mark next to Antarctica as well. Jerry boasted and strutted around with his chest puffed up so often that I'm fairly certain had a particular diminutive Frenchman never been born, there would still be a complex dubbed The Jerry Greer Syndrome to describe the vertically challenged with aggrieved attitudes.

It was painfully obvious that most of Jerry's stories were blatant lies. He claimed to have spent ten years in the army, eight years in prison, and twelve as a plumber. The fact he was only thirty-four made the tales all the more ridiculous, but in a rare moment of quick thinking on his part, he answered Doyle's challenge with, "They sent me to military prison for attacking a general, and I worked as a plumber at Leavenworth."

That was Jerry. The human version.

Our customers didn't always have the ready cash to purchase what they needed, and Doyle was a natural horse-trader. So it wasn't unusual for him to swap and barter away our goods for something he considered of equal or greater value.

A fifty-pound sack of rabbit pellets for an old automatic chicken plucker. A small riding tractor for ten bags of fertilizer and a push-behind spreader. A rusty old stock tank for a few bales of alfalfa. Doyle would take anything if he thought he could resell it for a profit, but by far the most-swapped commodities were live animals.

Ducks, geese, rabbits, dogs.

Chickens, goats, miniature horses, pigeons.

Quail, pheasants, llamas.

Pigs, potbellied and otherwise.

We acquired and resold them all at one time or another. And that was exactly how Little Jerry came to the store. No, I'm not talking about Jerry Greer, my braggadocios coworker. I'm talking about Little Jerry, the Bantam Rooster.

Doyle traded a bottle of Malathion, a liquid insecticide mostly used to control mosquitoes, for the angry little bird. Actually, he'd traded for half a dozen or so chickens, but Little Jerry was the only one that earned a name. He did so by strutting around the yard and crowing all day long. The swaggering fowl fought, or fornicated with, any- and everything that moved from goats on down to leaves blowing in the wind.

Human Jerry despised the diminutive bird and cursed under his breath every time Doyle called it Little Jerry. The boss, however, loved the pugnacious bantam. So much so, he refused to sell him.

Long about July of that summer, Doyle made another trade. For a capon. A capon is a castrated rooster. Capons grow to twice their normal size and are often shown by 4-H and FFA kids. But stock show season had come and gone and it was several months away from county fair time, so this particular capon was destined for the frying pan, as it wasn't good for much else. Actually, it should've been butchered several months back as it had grown much larger and fatter than normal for a show animal. Doyle took one look at the oversized bird and dubbed it Little Travis.

He'd had so much fun comparing the capricious cock to Jerry, he couldn't resist naming this oaf of a clucker after me. The capon must have been twelve or thirteen pounds—the size of a young turkey.

Man has often debated which came first, the chicken or the egg, but Little Jerry and Little Travis spawned a new philosophical question. Did Doyle decide to instigate a fight between the human Jerry and Travis before or after he waged a cock fight between the fowls bearing our names? The chickens went beak-to-beak first. That much is a fact. But I'm not certain Doyle didn't set that battle up as an undercard to the main event.

Many of our customers raised and fought gamecocks. Matter of fact, Doyle was a silent partner in several ventures and often went over to Clovis, New Mexico, to watch and wager upon the cockfights. Back in those days, cockfighting was legal in every state that bordered Texas. Despite the activity being against the law, owners and trainers could spar their birds without repercussion within the borders of The Lone Star State, as long as the birds incurred no harm.

In order to do this, padded leather pouches were tied around each of the cock's legs. The pouches, or muffs as they were called, covered the sharp bony spur which naturally grew on their legs. This kept the birds from doing any actual damage to each other while letting them practice, and Pearl's just happened to stock the sparring muffs.

A few days after we acquired Little Travis, one of the store regulars, a cockfighter and saddle maker named Willie Roebuck took one look at the capon and said, "That's a big fucking chicken. Reckon it could get its fat ass up in the air and shuffle?"

Shuffling is what the cockfighters called it when the birds pumped their legs to rake their spurs into their fellow combatant. Ideally a bird would do this while flying higher in the air than his opponent, since doing so made him much more likely to survive.

"Doubt it," Doyle said. "I got a banty rooster out back that would kick his big ass in nothing flat."

"Ain't no banty gonna hurt that big bastard," Willie said. "Not naked heeled, anyway."

"Naked heel" was the term used when birds were pitted against each other with only their spurs as weapons. In other types of fights, knives or gaffs were tethered to the cock's legs.

Ten minutes later, I was sent out to fetch Little Jerry. No easy task, given the rooster's surly attitude.

A large chalk circle about six feet in diameter was drawn onto the store's concrete floor, and a pair of sparring muffs were attached to each of the birds. Though in truth, the capon barely had any spurs in the first place.

Doyle wagered a hundred dollars that Little Travis would either run out of the circle, or be knocked out by the much cockier and smaller bird. Displaying faith in the larger bird, Willie matched the bet, adamant that Little Travis would walk away the victor.

The first bird to be knocked from, or run out of, the circle would be declared the loser.

Jerry whispered back and forth with Doyle for a few minutes and then offered to bet me a twenty his namesake would whip mine. I was reluctant to take the bet. Despite his name, I felt no loyalty to the capon. However, Doyle wasn't about to let me slide. "Come on. What's twenty bucks?"

"About five hours' wages around here," I answered.

"Don't be puss. You big guys should stick up for each other."

"You're as big as I am. Why don't you bet on the capon?"

Jerry folded his arms across his puffed-up chest and grinned. "Cause he ain't stupid. Doyle knows size don't mean shit. Especially when you got no balls."

The boss laughed. "You talking about the capon, or Big Travis?"

"Not much difference between 'em if he's too scared to bet."

I reached in my wallet and pulled out a twenty. "At least I didn't have to whisper in Doyle's ear to borrow money."

Pissed that I'd let them goad me into what I feared was a losing proposition, I glanced at Willie, who flashed me a crooked grin. "Don't worry. We both just made some easy cash."

Right from the start, it looked bleak for both Little Travis and my twenty bucks. The second the two birds were released, Little Jerry went after his much larger foe. For a good thirty seconds the bantam-weight bad-ass laid into the capon.

Feathers flew.

Legs spurred.

Wings flapped.

The big white capon simply stood and took his flogging until the other bird tired. Out of wind, but still angry, Little Jerry circled his opponent with one wing lowered to the ground in a posturing act of aggression, but still Little Travis did nothing.

Grinning broadly, Doyle said, "Told you that little banty would kick his ass."

Willie Roebuck shook his head. "That Capon ain't hurt. All that shuffling. Ain't moved an inch. No way he's gonna get knocked out of the circle, and he ain't ran yet."

"Damned thing's too stupid to run," Jerry chimed in.

"Let's pick 'em up and pit them again," Willie said.

Doyle scooped up Little Jerry. The angry bird immediately latched his beak onto the loose skin of Doyle's hand. Willie picked up Little Travis, who again did nothing more than stare out at the world with dull, yellow eyes. The two men faced each other holding the birds in their hands. Extending their arms they brought the roosters close together three times before again setting them on the ground. Little Jerry resumed his relentless assault with the exact same result.

Three, four, five times. We repeated the ritual. Actually, the delay between the third and fourth was a good bit longer, as a customer showed up and we had to wait until Doyle sold her a box of snail granules before the next round could commence.

"Shit," Doyle said after the fifth go-around. "This could go on all day. That Capon ain't phased by getting his ass kicked, and he sure as hell doesn't seem interested in fighting back."

Jerry smirked at me. "'Cause he's got no balls."

"Let's call it a tie," Doyle said.

"Hell, no." Willie picked up Little Travis. "Your bird will have a heart attack and die before it wins. I'll let you off for fifty right now if you wanna quit, but we ain't settling for no tie."

"Nope," I said feeling better about the wager. "I don't think that capon even realizes he's in a fight." I stared back at human Jerry. "Then again, neither would I if an angry midget attacked me."

Six, seven, eight. Nothing changed.

Must have been the ninth or tenth time before Little Travis finally had enough. The bantam attacked, and just like all the times before, he eventually tired and resorted to making those slow shuffling circles around his enemy. That's when Little Travis reared back and shuffled one time.

It wasn't pretty. And his butt never got off the ground, but the kick sent Little Jerry sliding across the concrete floor. He landed a good five feet away. Beneath a shelving unit.

And he stayed there. Doyle tried to pull the bird out, but the bantam was having none of it. He pecked and squawked each time the boss touched him.

"Might as well leave him there," Willie gloated. "Our bird already won." He scooped his hundred up off the counter and, now pleased that I'd taken the bet, I did the same with Jerry's twenty.

But Doyle hated to lose. He only stared as Willie exited the store with a smile on his face. Turning his attention back on the defeated bantam, he said, "Bet that's what it would look like if you two went to blows. Jerry you would be throwing a shitload of worthless punches, and then all of a sudden Travis would knock the piss out of you."

"Shit." Jerry ran the back of his hand across his nose. "I've whooped guys a hell of a lot bigger than him."

Doyle finally grabbed the bantam's legs and yanked him out from his hiding place. The bird dangled from the boss's hand, as a slow grin spread across his face.

I should've known right then Doyle would never rest until Jerry and I settled our beef the old fashioned way.

Chapter Ten

Cage Fight

Only days after the cockfight, Doyle sold Little Jerry to a shriveled old Mexican lady for a mere three bucks. A regular named Hong bought Little Travis a week or so later. To many of our Laotian and Vietnamese customers, Pearl's was as much a live meat market as anything else.

So, Little Travis won the battle, but lost the war when he was served upon a bed of sticky rice. Little Jerry, on the other hand, lived out his days guarding Mrs. Reynosa's backyard and servicing her hens.

Meanwhile, the war at Pearl's raged on between the human Jerry and myself. By the end of July, battle lines had been drawn. Our animosity for each other grew with every day, and with every task we were forced to endure in each other's company—like unloading a large shipment of alfalfa hay. Each bale weighed in excess of eighty pounds and we'd been at it over an hour, when I paused to catch my breath.

Jerry shook his head and muttered just loud enough for

me to hear, "Never would have cut it in the Army. Woulda washed out in boot camp."

Of course he was up on the flat bed trailer pushing the bales off onto the ground, whereas I was assigned to pick them up and stack 'em in the upper reaches of the metal hay barn. Suffocating heat gathered at the top of the barn and made it at least a hundred and ten, even on the cooler days. The mercury in that particular location could rise well above 140 degrees or more on a sweltering Texas afternoon.

"Look at you sweating. Young guy like you oughtta be in better shape. This ain't even real heat. You want hot? Try marching twenty miles through the jungles of 'Nam."

"You could swap with me and try stacking for a while."

"Could," Jerry smirked. "But I got seniority. Now get your ass back to work."

"When I'm good and ready," I said.

Jerry harked up a wad of phlegm. The mucous ball flew by, only inches from my head. "That kind of talk will get you shanked in prison," he said.

My back ached, my arms hurt, and sweat stung my eyes. I was in no mood to listen to Jerry's tales of prison or military bravado. "Yeah, well, I'm not a dumbass, so I don't plan on ever going to prison. Unless it's for choking the shit out of you the next time your spit lands anywhere near me."

Every once in a while, Doyle would stick his head out the door of the air-conditioned store and yell for us to hurry the hell up. Being summer, his boys were out of school and running around terrorizing the joint as usual. At the moment they were off playing in the vacant field across the street from Pearl's. The field was a good seven or eight acres of nothing more than broken up slabs of concrete and yellow, waist-high weeds, but at least the boys were not inside the store tearing crap up, or creating another mess I'd have to clean.

Jerry and I managed to unload the more than four hundred bales by early afternoon without killing each other. Being payday Friday, he was itching to leave early. After he repaid Doyle for all the advances during the week, Jerry's paychecks never amounted to more than a hundred bucks or so. Nevertheless, he would take whatever cash he got and head off to the bars, in search of a good buzz and a skanky companion. Come Saturday morning he'd show up looking and smelling like death warmed over, with some tale about the hot babe he'd picked up at Vaqueros, The Cattleman, or some other dive over on Amarillo Boulevard.

Doyle counted out Jerry's pay and then let him have the rest of the day off. By late afternoon it was just the boss, me, and his three boys, who were still over in the field doing only-God-knows-what.

Steve Golds showed up right at closing time. I hadn't seen him in over a month. Not since the party out at the Bailloux's, after John and Candy's graduation. Steve and I had always been more like friends of a friend than anything else, so I was surprised when he said, "Thought I'd stop by and see what you've been up to."

"Not much. Just working."

"Working hell," Doyle chimed in. "More like stealing. All he does is sit around here in the cool air-conditioning waiting to get paid."

When Doyle walked outside to whistle for his boys, Steve said, "He seems like a decent boss. This a cool place to work?"

"Beats flipping burgers," I answered.

"Or roofing houses with your dad."

Steve's dad owned a roofing company. Steve, John Bailloux, and a couple of other guys, worked for him every summer. They earned more money than I did, but worked a hell of a lot harder for it, as well.

"John told me you like to fish. I was thinking about heading up to Meredith tonight to see if the walleye are biting. Wanna come?"

"I would, but last time I went with John he wanted to stay all night and I gotta work in the morning."

Steve shook his head. "John's working with Brent at the Blue Beacon tonight. It's just me and we'll be home by midnight. But we gotta take your truck, I'm nearly outta gas and my dad's holding my check."

"What for?"

Steve dismissed my question with a wave of his hand. "It's bullshit, but he's pissed off about some stuff and thinks I need to be saving money. So you in?"

I understood the deal. Steve couldn't go unless he found

somebody to take him. But I didn't have anything else going, and Steve was a decent enough guy. Besides, there were worse ways to spend a Friday night than on the banks of a lake with a fishing pole in your hand.

"Yeah, I'll swing home to grab my stuff. Pick you up about seven."

"Cool, bring some beer if you can."

When I explained my plans, and asked Doyle to buy me a twelve pack, he simply stuck his hand out for the money. When he returned from the liquor store, he said, "Fishing. When I was your age I spent Friday nights out chasing pussy. But no, you and your buddy would rather sit around together and play with your worms. Hell, even Jerry is out getting drunk and chasing hoes. Ugly, fat hoes, but at least his fingers will smell like fish for the right damn reason."

By eight we'd arrived at the lake and hiked out to my favorite spot at the end of a rocky point. Lake Meredith was basically a rocky, tree-deprived canyon that had been dammed.

On good years, when there had been some rainfall, the Canadian river filled the lake with red muddy water, but drought or not, the wind nearly always blew hard enough to create whitecaps on the waves.

Once we got our lines cast out into the choppy waters, Steve asked, "You going to Brent's wedding?"

"Yeah, I'm supposed to be an usher!" What with the waves slapping the rocks and the wind whistling by, I had to holler three times before Steve heard me, so conversation was sparse for the next hour.

By dusk, we'd only caught one ten-inch sand bass that we debated keeping, but eventually tossed back. I'd also hooked a small, probably undersized walleye, but it had shaken off my hook before I got it into the bank. As the sun disappeared behind our backs, the wind finally subsided. We'd drunk three or four beers apiece by that time, so life was good even if the fishing wasn't.

"Heard from Candy?" I asked.

It was fairly common knowledge that Steve had been hung up on her, despite her adventurous ways. He'd even tried to talk her into staying in Amarillo, but her mind was made up.

"Nope. John told me she's only called home once." Cracking open another Coors Light, he looked at me, "You talked to Missy?"

"No. And I hope it stays that way."

Steve laughed. "I get you. She doesn't quite compare to Candy."

An hour later the only bites we'd had were from a variety of bugs that swarmed once the wind died. The twelve pack was gone and the only sounds around the lake were the hum of some far off oil pump and the steady drone of bullfrogs.

"When's Brent's baby due?" Steve asked.

"October. But Lisa is already showing."

"August, September, October. Three months," he said.

It was dark enough that I couldn't really see Steve as he counted off the months.

"Sherry's pregnant too," I said.

"You're shitting me?"

I reeled in my line to see if the minnow on my hook was still alive. "Nope, due in December."

"Never pegged her as a girl who put out. Her and Curtis gonna get married too?"

"Probably." I pulled a wad of green algae off my hook and rebaited. "Brent, Cherry, Suzy, Jamie. If you count both Cole and Crystal, that makes six kids in our AG class that are about to have a kid of their own. Maybe they ought to take animal husbandry out of the curriculum." I laughed.

Steve didn't join in. Instead he said, "Actually, seven. If you count me."

"You?"

"Fuck, yeah." He picked up one of his poles.

Far as I knew, Steve didn't even have a girlfriend. Unless you counted Candy, but she was gone.

"Not Candy," I said.

"I wish," Steve answered as he cranked his reel. "But you know she didn't go that far. No way was she gonna to let some dude knock her up. She was too hell-bent on heading off to Florida."

I waited while Steve dug a fresh minnow from the bucket, but he recasted and sat back down on a large rock without elaborating.

"You gonna tell me who?"

Somewhere off to our right a fish jumped. The sound of the splash had faded before he finally answered. "Summer."

"Summer Johnson?"

"Hell, yeah. She kept asking me to take her for a ride in my Mustang. One night I got pissed off at Candy and thought, what the hell. Summer told me she was on the pill. You know how many guys have done her. I figured she was telling the truth. Otherwise she'd have a dozen kids by now."

Summer Johnson had a reputation as a plan B girl. Whenever anybody's date went bad, or they were just particularly itching for a good time, they went to see Summer.

"Y'all dating?" I asked.

"Hell no, and we damn sure ain't getting married. But she wants to keep the baby, so I gotta keep working for my dad to pay my share."

"You won't be able to work for your dad when you move to Brenham."

Steve had earned a baseball scholarship to a school down in south Texas. He was one of the few kids I knew going away for college.

"I'm not going. Lost my scholarship and now my dad says I can keep my ass here and go to AC."

"Sucks about the baseball. But Amarillo College won't be too bad. That's probably where I'll be next year."

"Maybe, but I'll be stuck in Amarillo," he said. "One dumbass move. Candy was right. Now I'm trapped. Should've been happy with her blowjobs. Or wrapped it up when I took Summer for that ride."

The fishing never got any better so Steve and I went home around eleven. Nevertheless, I was still tired come the next day, and Saturday mornings were our busiest time. That particular Saturday was no exception, and Doyle did little more than stand around with a coffee mug in his hand, telling stories even though Jerry hadn't shown.

Luckily, the boys spent the morning over in the field across the street and didn't create any messes for me to clean. Customers trickled off by late morning, but when the mailman made his delivery, it included three boxes of baby chicks, turkeys, and pheasants, so I stayed busy getting their cages ready.

I'd just gotten our latest collection of fuzzy little chicks settled when the boys triumphantly returned from across the street with a three-and-a-half foot long bull snake. They'd caught it slithering through the weeds and rubble. The writhing reptile was not pleased with its fate. Austin clutched the snake behind its gaping, hissing mouth while Dallas held the belly. Doyle's youngest, Houston, tried to hold the tail but that end kept slipping through the youngster's grubby little hands. Doyle joined the boys in tormenting the pissed off reptile for a while, but the real fun started when he spotted Jerry pulling into the narrow strip of asphalt we called a parking lot. He was only five hours late, but no doubt my coworker would have one hell of a bullshit story to justify his tardiness.

"You guys wanna scare the shit out of Jerry?" Doyle asked.

"Yeah," all three boys answered.

Doyle kept his focus on Jerry's dilapidated station wagon as he said, "Hurry. Go stick that snake in the bulk hen scratch bin. Make sure the latch catches so it can't get out."

Jerry slithered in a few seconds later looking like he was the one who had just crawled from beneath a rock. His thatch of black hair was ratted and askew. His clothes, the same ones he'd left the store in yesterday afternoon, were wrinkled and filthy. A large gash on his forearm still oozed blood.

Reaching for his timecard, which we filled out ourselves, Jerry said, "Sorry about this morning, but you ain't gonna believe what happened to me."

"Let me guess," Doyle said. "You picked up some fat gal at Cattleman's last night. She handcuffed you to her bed and then left you there this morning when she went to The Waffle House to chow down on grits and sausage. You'd just started gnawing your own arm off to escape when she came home and set you free. But only after you promised to deliver another helping of Russell, The One-Eyed Love Muscle."

Jerry took a seat at one of the stools. "You ain't that far off. Except she wasn't fat, and she didn't handcuff me. She did steal my car keys so I couldn't leave until she came back. I broke the window of my car thinking I left my keys in it. Cut my fucking arm on the glass, but that's okay. Betty nursed me back to health."

I wondered if that was the story Jerry originally planned to tell or a version he concocted as Doyle told his.

The boss scowled. "So me and Travis have been busting ass here at work while you was off getting a piece from some fat gal named Betty?"

"She wasn't fat."

"And now you come in here and plop your lazy ass down on a stool with this bullshit story." Doyle shook his head. "Maybe Travis is right. Maybe I should shit can you."

"I—" I tried to speak, knowing Jerry would immediately believe I was trying to get him fired.

"I tried to defend you," Doyle said cutting me off. "But fuck it's getting harder and harder every day."

Doyle was practically smiling now. Not that Jerry noticed. He was too busy glaring at me. There was no need for me to point out I hadn't said a thing about the boss firing Jerry. My coworker had already made up his mind. If I tried to proclaim my innocence, Doyle would only sell the notion harder.

"Don't just sit there giving Travis that go-to-hell look," Doyle said. "There's work to be done. Go sack up ten pounds of hen scratch for Old Lady Schmidt. She's on her way to pick it up."

When Jerry stomped out of the room, Doyle practically knocked me down getting to the intercom. He turned the volume all the way up, already grinning from ear to ear.

One loud "MOTHERFUCKER!" was followed by a series of crashes, bangs, and undecipherable cusses. After that nothing but laughter as the boys erupted from wherever they'd been hiding to watch.

Doyle and I hurried back to the feed room where we found Jerry trying to untangle himself from an old set of grain scales. His arm was bleeding worse, and he now had an additional scratch across his left cheek.

"Y'all put that fucking snake in there, didn't you?"

Our laughter answered his question. But while we were enjoying Jerry's misery, the snake slithered out of the feed bin and disappeared.

We spent the rest of the afternoon looking for the escapee to no avail. The boys were bummed their prey had disappeared, and Jerry refused to so much as step foot in the sack room until the thing was found. That meant I carried out every last sack of feed that afternoon.

The store was closed on Sunday, and Monday morning it was my turn to come dragging in late. Just fifteen minutes or so, not anywhere near as tardy as Jerry had been the Saturday before, but tardy enough to bring out the righteous side of my coworker.

Like I said, we filled out our own time cards. Each day I wrote down seven thirty as my start time and six as my end time. Most mornings, I didn't actually show up until seven forty-five or so, but we rarely left at straight up six. More like six-thirty. And yet, I wrote six at the end of each day. But fresh off of Doyle's comment about my thinking he should fire Jerry, my coworker clearly wanted to make a point.

He snatched up my time card the moment I slipped it

back in the holder. Sizing it up he said, "What's this shit? You wasn't here at no seven-thirty today."

"Mind your own business," I replied.

Doyle was leaned against the counter, looking eager for an argument.

"It is my business," Jerry blurted. "I depend on this place for a living and you're cheating the company."

"Company?" I said. "There are three of us. That hardly makes a company, but don't worry, I'll still write down six tonight. Even when I have to stay late."

I didn't care to hear what else Jerry had to say, so I headed back to the chick room to perform my daily duties. That's when I found the missing snake.

Turns out a three-and-a half foot bull snake with an empty gut can squeeze through places that a snake with a bellyful of baby chicks cannot and it had certainly done its best to eat as many chicks as possible.

I hollered to Doyle to come and see.

Shaking his head, either at the carnage, lost revenue, or maybe both, Doyle simply said, "Shit."

Peering between our shoulders, Jerry whispered, "See what you sick bastards caused?"

Using a small, three-pronged garden fork to pin the snake against the wire, Doyle yanked the fat reptile out of the cage. He cut off its head with a hatchet and tossed the carcass in the dumpster. The boys had spent the night with some cousin, so this time they were not around to turn the decapitated critter into a plaything. The rest of the morning passed smoothly. Until lunch.

Doyle always went first, about ten thirty or so. When he returned, sometime around noon, Jerry would go. I always went last. We were supposed to take an hour, but like most things around Pearl's, the rules were somewhat lax.

Jerry had left at straight up noon. By ten after one, he still wasn't back.

That's when Doyle started in on me. "Hey, when Jerry comes back and fills out his time card, I want you to grab it and start bitching because he only claimed an hour lunch."

"Why?"

"Why not? He was jacking with you this morning about being late."

"Doesn't matter," I pointed out. "If not that, he'd just find something else to gripe about."

"So? You can't let him fuck with you or it will just get worse. You gotta keep little pricks like him in check. Otherwise they get too cocky." Doyle pointed outside. "Here he comes."

Just as Doyle knew he would, Jerry wrote down twelve to one, despite the fact it was now fifteen after. However, I'm not sure even Doyle anticipated the full extent of the explosion when I grabbed his time sheet and loudly pointed out Jerry's error.

"Fuck you, you wet-behind-the-ears motherfucker! I ain't gonna put up with you going behind me back checking my work or crying to the boss trying to get me fired!"

"But you don't mind checking my time card?"

"I'm the god-damned warehouse manager! I'm supposed to keep you line."

"You tell him, Jerry." Doyle looked at me, obviously eager to hear my comeback.

"You can't even keep yourself in line. Much less keep me from anything."

"I can damn sure drag your ass out to the alley and teach you a fucking lesson."

Jerry had made the threat before. I'd never taken the bait, but I'd come to realize we were destined to have it out sooner or later. Now seemed as good a time as any.

"Let's go," I said.

I moved toward the garage door that opened to the alley.

A customer pulled up out front.

"Now's not the time." Jerry pointed out to the still-idling car.

"Sure it is," Doyle chimed in. "Y'all go ahead. I'll get rid of them and be right out."

"Fine," Jerry muttered. "He wants an ass kicking." Jerry raised a fist. "I'll give it to him."

I'd been in a few fights over the years, mostly back in elementary school when we boys got ticked off over a game of football-turned-too rough, or some taunt gone too far. I'd even been in one or two back in junior high, but those had been against boys my own age. Or thereabouts. As Jerry yanked the chain to raise the garage door, I couldn't help be somewhat nervous. He was after all a grown man, nearly two decades older than myself. Plus, he spent his days tossing around heavy feed sacks. But so did I, I told myself. I was both bigger and stronger than him and, well, there comes a time when you have to man up. See if you're tough enough to hack it.

The door opened. My time had arrived.

We stepped out into the sunshine. Shards of broken bottles glittered along the dirt alley. I balled my hands into fists and took a step toward Jerry.

He backed away.

"Thought you wanted to teach me a lesson," I said.

Jabbing a finger toward my face, he said, "Now's not the time or place, but someday, somewhere, you're gonna look up and find me in your face. And you won't like it when that day arrives." And with that, Jerry turned and walked away. Straight out to his car, which he promptly got in and drove off.

Needless to say, Doyle was highly disappointed. He made me tell him the story a dozen times and when Jerry showed up the next day acting like nothing had ever happened, Doyle pounced.

For two or three days straight he badgered Jerry with a constant barrage of, "Is this the day? How 'bout the time?" or he'd break out in song, singing "Somewhere over the rainbow, I'll find a place not to be a pussy." There were, of course, more lyrics, but you get the idea.

Tuesday. Wednesday. Thursday. Doyle taunted Jerry nonstop. Come Friday morning Jerry didn't show. That in itself wasn't unusual, but when he failed to come in for a second day Doyle grew concerned. That evening the boss talked me into riding along to the trailer park where Jerry rented a battered old mobile home. The front door was flapping in the breeze and a dozen or so cats basked in the evening sun. Jerry was nowhere to be found. The place smelled like the giant litter box it was and appeared to have been ransacked, but Doyle claimed it always looked that way. A neighbor came out and informed us, Jerry had loaded up his car with everything it would hold and took off a few nights ago, saying he wouldn't be back.

Upon our return to the feed store Doyle said, "Wonder what makes a guy just take off like that?"

But I knew. Doyle never would have let Jerry live down the fact he'd walked away from that fight. Jerry had felt trapped.

Like a teenage boy with a baby on the way.

Like a snake in a cage.

Chapter Eleven

More Than You're Willing To Give

Doyle decided not to replace Jerry. That meant I spent lots of time alone at the store during Doyle's trips to see his lawyer, his long, extended lunch breaks, and of course, the conjugal visits to whatever gal he happened to be trifling with at the time. The boss's bargain with Tasha was ongoing, though after I ruined her fun, it took several months before she came sashaying back. Still ticked off that Doyle refused to fire me, she made it LOUD and clear that I was a low-life, perverted douche bag. Though, it turns out, neither Doyle nor myself had seen the full force of Tasha's fury.

Tasha had been working off her feed tab the better part of a year when in strolled a man. Doyle was at lunch, so I was manning the joint by myself. I didn't recognize the fella as one of our regular customers, so I was a might surprised when he stepped up to the counter and said, "I'm here to pay off my charge account."

"What's the name?" I asked.

"Jones. Seth Jones."

I didn't recognize the name anymore than I had his face, and when I searched through the alphabetized slips pinned to the corkboard I couldn't find a tally sheet under that name.

"Might be under my wife's name," the guy finally added. "She usually picks up the feed on her way home from work. Her name is Tasha … "

Forget the proverbial deer in the headlights. I must have looked like a Southern Baptist preacher caught by his congregation with a *Penthouse* in one hand and a fifth of Jim Beam in the other. Guilt-ridden heat colored my cheeks, and I wasn't even the one who'd spent the last year back in the feed room banging his wife.

Gaining some semblance of composure I said, "Doyle has a screwed-up filing system. Sometimes only he can figure it out, but if you come back in an hour or so he'll be back from lunch."

I should've told the dude two hours, because as it happened, Doyle and Tasha's husband returned at the exact same time. I'd hoped to warn my boss, but that possibility went out the window when they walked into the store one after the other, Doyle holding the door for the man.

The boss took one look at my worried expression and frowned. "What's up?"

"This is Tasha's husband. He came in earlier to pay her tab, but I couldn't find their account on the board."

The word husband didn't faze Doyle in the least. He simply strolled over to the corkboard behind the counter, flipped through a couple of tally sheets, and calmly yanked one down.

Doyle punched a few buttons on the cash register before announcing, "Adds up to three-hundred eight-nine dollars, and sixty-nine cents." Doyle shot me a wink, while the other man reached for his checkbook.

Tasha's husband nodded and began filling out the check. "I didn't think she was paying the bill often enough. I give her the cash every month, but who knows what she does with the money. Surprised we don't owe more."

"Would be higher," Doyle said. "Except I give Tasha a discount. She's one of our favorite customers."

The man grinned. "Appreciate it. Those damn horses cost enough to support as is. Pretty sure they eat better I do."

The man took his receipt and headed out the door without another comment.

I simply stared at Doyle until the boss shrugged his shoulders and said, "What?"

"You, are an evil man. Steal a man's wife and his money."

"I didn't steal a thing. He's still got his wife, and his horses ate the grain his check just paid for."

I raised a brow.

"Am I wrong?"

"Not technically," I said.

"So in actuality I did John-Boy there a favor. I extended him a line of interest-free credit, and I kept both his horses and his wife fat and happy in the process. Hell, I shoulda charged him a commission for the extra services I've provided."

Doyle could present a reasonable argument to defend just about any of his actions. He'd have made a damn fine defense attorney.

"Was that even Tasha's ticket?" I asked. "Or the right amount?"

"It was in the ballpark, but I should've tossed out a larger number. He would've paid it. But I wasn't sure how high John-Boy would go without making a fuss. I knew he'd be a dork, but that ol' boy ain't been off the farm much."

Tasha hit the store maybe an hour later. "What the fuck, Doyle?" The door hadn't even swung shut behind her before she was at the counter pointing a long, neon-green nail in the boss's face.

His expression never changed.

"How could you?" She demanded.

"How could I what?" His voice was nice and even, but I could tell by the way he slowly leaned back, away from Tasha, that Doyle recognized the potential dangers of the situation.

"You know damn good and well what." The fat ringlets of hair encircling Tasha's face bounced and swayed along with her plump skull. Until then, I'd thought only angry, black women and Jerry Springer guests were capable of making that slow rolling motion with their head.

Now that he was far enough back from the counter to be out of arm's reach, Doyle grinned. "What did you want me to do? Tell him his wife already worked off the debt? The man came in expecting to owe me money. I merely gave him what he wanted."

I laughed.

Out loud.

Both Doyle and Tasha shot me hate-filled looks, but I had to say it. "Something tells me he never wanted you to bone his wife."

"You," Tasha turned her gaudily adorned finger on me, "can shut the fuck up."

I bit down on my lip to keep from completely losing my composure. Needless to say, I was enjoying the scene.

Tasha refocused her ire upon Doyle. "Fine. You had to tell him something. Now give me the cash."

The boss shook his head. "John-Boy didn't pay with cash. He wrote a check."

"His name is Seth."

With much effort I resisted my ever-so-strong urge to say, *Oh, how sweet of you to defend your husband's good name.*

"So give me the check." Her tone carried the air of a threat.

"I would." Doyle sucked in air. "But my dad swung by on his way to the bank. I'm afraid it's already been deposited."

Tasha threw the Folgers can full of peanuts first. Doyle managed to raise one arm, but the metal container clung painfully off of his left elbow as nuts flew everywhere. Call me a chicken if you will, but I slipped out and fled to the feed room when she reached for a bottle of liquid pesticide.

"Damn it, Tasha. Don't—"

The shattering of glass cut Doyle's words off. I peeked around the corner to see if any shards were imbedded in his skull just in time to see Doyle hop the counter and grab Tasha in a bear hug. Yet another bottle dangled in her hand.

Pinned as her arms were she couldn't do much, but she tried. Eventually she dropped the second bottle, which promptly shattered at their feet.

"If you leave now," Doyle said between clenched teeth, "I'll forget you came by, but I can't have you destroying any more of my shit. Or disrupting my business."

"I loved you," Tasha sobbed.

"I know you did." Doyle lowered his voice to the point I couldn't hear what he said, but after only a few seconds the anger seemed to drain from her body.

Doyle let her go.

She stood there, her shoulders shaking as she sobbed.

Now it was Doyle's turn to escape. He hurried toward me mouthing the word "Go" as he approached. Together we slipped back to the feed room. I started to speak, but the boss put a finger to his lips and whispered, "Shhh."

We sat down on the sacks of feed and waited. I couldn't help but note it hadn't been all that long since Doyle and Tasha had been back here in an entirely different embrace than the one I'd just witnessed. Maybe five minutes elapsed before an engine started out front. Ten seconds later, we heard Tasha drive away.

Doyle stood and said, "That went better than I thought."

"Better?"

"Yeah, I wasn't sure how I was gonna get rid of her before John-Boy rolled in today." We walked back up front where Doyle promptly handed me a broom. "She'd been getting too clingy. Asking me questions about who else I was dating. If I ever planned to get married again."

I swept the broken shards of Tasha's anger into the dustpan Doyle was holding.

"I was starting to get worried she would leave old John-Boy," he said. "The last thing I wanted was to look up and find Tasha standing on my porch holding her suitcases."

"You still might."

"Nah. I told her she deserved someone better than a two-timing asshole like me. And she believed it. She'll buy her horse feed somewhere else from now on. I guarantee it."

"Until she can't pay the bill," I pointed out.

Doyle paused. His hand only inches from dumping the glass into the trash can, he looked back at me and said, "I thought I'd taught you a few things. It was never about her not having the money."

"You're telling me she made that part up just to seduce you? Doesn't she know a horn-dog like you simply needs an invitation?"

"Son, son, son. Will you ever learn? Tasha didn't come here just to get her jollies off. John-Boy could've taken care of that at home. To hear her tell it he's hung like a damned horse.

But he's too freakin' nice. Buys her flowers every week and shit. Women never want what they already have, and Tasha had a husband that treated her nice. Like a lady. She came to see me so she could feel like a whore. You think I left the intercom on just so you could sit up here and jerk off. Hell no. I left it on because it made Tasha feel dirty." Doyle sat at his throne behind the counter and laced his fingers together behind his head. "Yep, you gotta give 'em what they want, unless of course they want more than you're willing to give. That's when you have to cut them loose."

Over the coming days I pondered Doyle's advice. *Give 'em what they want.* Seemed reasonable enough, except I rarely had a clue what girls my age wanted, and the things I did know were beyond my control. Samantha Blake obviously wanted an older guy. That was all she ever dated, anyway. And I damn sure couldn't change the year I was born. So knowing her wants did me no good.

Unless they want more than you're willing to give.

I thought about that statement, as well. To be honest, I wasn't willing to give much. Maybe even nothing. From what I'd seen of relationships, giving anything at all created nothing but trouble. Most of my friends from school were expecting a kid. Doyle had knocked up two different women, which had resulted in three separate divorces at that time. I'd just witnessed a crazy woman try to bash in his skull after he'd given her exactly what she wanted. Then there was my own parents' miserable relationship. They'd been divorced for a number of years, but I couldn't recall a single moment of happiness involving both of them. Not even from earliest memories as a little kid. All I could remember was my mom giving him chance after chance to stay away from the whiskey.

With those facts flying through my noggin I'd began the final descent into Jadedville International when Doyle asked me, "What you got going after work tomorrow night?"

"Why?"

"Got a can't-miss proposition for you."

I stared at Doyle, waiting for him to elaborate.

"I'm gonna pay for you to go out on a date. With Delinda's daughter. She's sixteen. Goes to Amarillo High. Her name's Macy, or Marcy, or something like that."

Delinda was the boss's latest plaything. She worked the window at his favorite burger joint. An old school greasy spoon over on old Route 66 that damn few ventured inside to eat at, but where a steady line of cars picked food up from the window. Sometimes it's better not to see the inner workings of things. It had taken him a while, but a month or so back he'd finally worn her down and gotten her to agree to a date. According to Doyle, that date had been hotter than a vat of boiling fry oil. He'd been buttering Delinda's buns ever since.

This was the first I'd heard of a daughter.

"Macy, huh. She must be big as one of those Thanksgiving floats if you gotta pay someone to take her out."

"No, she's a cute girl. Kind of morose, but cute."

I shot Doyle a dubious look.

"I'm not bullshitting you. Delinda caught her dry humping some dude on the couch and now she's convinced her daughter is a sex-crazed nympho. I had to really sell the fact you're a nice guy. Shy, naïve. Not the type to take advantage of her daughter. So make sure you shave that shit off your upper lip before Friday."

"I'm growing a mustache," I said.

"There are twelve-year-old girls with more fuzz on their twat than you have on your lip. Shave it off."

"I'm not doing it."

Doyle rolled his eyes. "It'll grow back. I already told Delinda you were a clean cut kid."

Shaking my head I said, "No. I mean I'm not taking her daughter out. I'm swearing off dating until I graduate."

The boss's eyes widened. "You're shittin' me, right? What are you, queer or something?"

"No. Smart. Three quarter of my friends are already expecting a kid, and the ones who aren't are broke anyway because their girlfriend wants them to buy 'em stuff or take them somewhere."

Now it was Doyle's turn to shoot me a dubious expression.

Feeling compelled to explain my position, I carried on. "And you've always got some kind of female trouble. If it's not an ex-wife trying to kill you, it's somebody throwing shit at you. Besides, you were the one who said to cut them loose once they start to want more than you're willing to give."

Doyle almost grinned, but still said nothing.

Continuing with my reasoning, I asked, "Why should I give anything, when the best looking girl in my grade refuses to go out with anyone her own damn age? And every other girl is either already pregnant or dating someone else? Or else has an evil, interfering little sister lurking around the corner? Huh? What the hell incentive do I have?"

Doyle only shrugged, but I could see he was trying hard not to laugh. The fact he found my tirade funny made me all the more determined not to take out Macy, or Marcy, or whatever the hell her name was.

"And now you wanna pawn your girlfriend's daughter off on me. Well," I folded my arms across my chest. "I'm not doing it."

The boss couldn't take it anymore. He burst into laughter.

"Laugh all you want. I'm not taking her out."

Once he regained control, Doyle said, "You need to get laid even worse than I thought."

I grabbed a broom and pushed it around the room, even though I'd swept the floor less than an hour ago.

"I'm not asking you to marry the girl," Doyle said. "I'm not even asking you to call her after Friday. I just need you to get her out of their apartment for a few hours. So I can have some fun. Her mom thinks it would set a bad example for us to slip off to the bedroom with her daughter watching TV in the other room."

"So take her to your trailer."

The boss shook his head. "I offered, but Delinda is afraid to leave the girl home alone. Or let her date." Doyle grinned. "But she's willing to make an exception for a nice kid like you."

"I'm not doing it."

"Come on," Doyle pleaded. "I need you to do this."

"No."

"I'm begging." Doyle folded his hands as if in prayer. "I'll give you a quarter an hour raise, pay all the costs for you to take her out, and give you any Saturday off you want."

I sat the broom aside and stared at him. "Tomorrow?"

"Yeah, tomorrow night," he answered.

"No, will you let me have tomorrow off?" It was the last Saturday of summer. The last Saturday before my senior year. The very last Saturday of the last summer before I graduated. The last summer Saturday of my childhood.

"Depends. Will you show up at my house by seven, so we can go over to Delinda's together?"

"I can't believe you're asking me to give up the last Saturday night of summer. To take out a girl I don't even know. Who most likely is some kind of freak. Who, even if she is cute, I have to act like some kind of friggin' boy scout around to impress her mother, and therefore come across as a complete dork to her."

"So you'll do it?"

No way in hell did I want to go on that date. And what was the point to having the day off if I had to show up at his house by seven?

I shook my head. "No. I'd rather have Saturday night to do what I want. The day will be ruined if I have to be at your house at seven."

"Okay," Doyle said. "Name your price. Go ahead. Bend me over and rape me. Tell me what it's gonna take for you to do me this one favor."

"Nothing. There's nothing you can do or offer that's going to change my mind."

"Every one has a price," he said.

"Not me. Not this time."

Doyle arched a brow. I hated it when he gave me that condescending look. As if he knew everything. As if he it was only a matter of time before I caved. But I was pissed. I wasn't going to let Doyle Suggs manipulate me. Not this time. So I said, "I'll stand buck-naked in the middle of the Amarillo Civic Center and sing *God Bless America* before I take your girlfriend's daughter out on a date."

Flash forward two nights. To the last Saturday of summer before my senior year. Oh, I was nude alright, but I wasn't at the Civic Center, and I sure wasn't singing *God Bless America*.

Chapter Twelve

God Bless America

Darcy.

That was her name. Not Macy. Not Marcy. Doyle hadn't even gotten the first letter correct, but to be fair, her mom did call her Darcy Marie, and if the lowcut blouse was an indication of Delinda's usual attire, Doyle's inability to hear properly in her presence was more than understandable.

Doyle had been correct about two things. One, Darcy was a cute girl. And two, she was morose. I suppose these days she would be described as goth, or at the very least emo, though neither of those terms had hit Amarillo, Texas, back in August of 1990. Darcy's skin was pale and her hair jet black, but she was definitely her mother's daughter. Darcy's inheritance was easy to see, even though her black Ramones t-shirt lacked the plunging neckline of Delinda's.

When Doyle introduced me, Darcy offered up a bland, "Hey," totally devoid of enthusiasm or emotion.

I smiled. Darcy didn't return the gesture. Her mom asked

me a few questions about school and work, which I answered while Darcy rolled her eyes.

After three or four minutes of small talk, the girl grabbed her purse off the coffee table and said, "I can't take anymore of this. Let's go if we're going."

"Be nice," her mom said.

"You kids have fun!" Doyle called out as we exited the apartment. "Don't do anything I wouldn't—"

Darcy slammed the door, cutting off his words. "Fuck off."

"I hope you were talking to him," I said.

"I can't stand any of my mom's boyfriends. They're all pricks, but he may be the worst."

"Doyle's not all bad."

"Easy for you to say. He's not fucking your mom."

Unsure how to respond, I led the way down the stairs and past the swimming pool. Heat radiated from the parking lot's black asphalt, making the splashes and squeals from the kids at the pool sound all the more inviting. Stopping alongside Doyle's faded S-10 Chevy pickup, I dug his keys from my pocket.

Darcy sighed. "We have to go in his piece of shit?" She arched a brow and shot me a disdainful look. "What, can't afford a ride of your own?"

Up in the apartment, for a few all-too-brief seconds, I'd thought maybe the date was going to turn out better than I'd imagined. Discovering Doyle had been right about Darcy being cute had been a pleasant surprise, but I was fast learning that while beauty was only skin deep, ugly went to the bone. And Darcy made no attempt to cover her skeletal structure.

Without looking at her I said, "I have a truck alright, but Doyle was afraid I'd dump you out at the first street corner and go my merry way if I drove my own vehicle."

I unlocked and opened the passenger door. Not as an act of chivalry, but because the driver's door was busted and only the inside latch worked. Reaching across, I pushed open the driver's door before standing aside to let Darcy sit.

"The air-conditioner in this thing better work."

The truck didn't actually have A/C, but I shut her door without relaying that info. She'd get the idea when I cranked down my window.

Before we'd even left the parking lot, Darcy whipped out a tube of lipstick. A deep burgundy, the color of congealed blood. Against her pale skin the makeup really stood out. Smacking her lips she said, "My mom hates this color. She told me not to wear it, but it's my *boyfriend's* favorite. My mom hates him, too."

Duly noting the heavy emphasis she put on the word boyfriend, I drove out of the lot without comment.

Three hours.

That was how much time I was obligated to spend. I didn't have a curfew, but Delinda had instructed me to have her daughter home by eleven. Far as I was concerned, ten was late enough, but part of the bargain with Doyle was to keep

Darcy Marie out as long as possible. Switching the radio from Doyle's standard country station to one that played rock music, she put her feet up on the dash. Neither fact bothered me. It wasn't my truck, and I enjoyed all kinds of tunes.

Outside, it was still better than ninety degrees, but Darcy hadn't rolled down her window. I was sweating, but then again I had on jeans, a button up shirt, and boots, whereas my date was wearing that thin Ramones t-shirt and a pair of shorts. Propped up as they were, I couldn't help but note the fact Darcy had damn nice legs. That fact alone gave me the incentive to try and get a conversation going.

"So, you're a junior this year?"

She nodded. "But I might drop out."

"Why?"

Rather than answer my question, she turned to face me. "What about you? What's your story? You work for Doyle but how did he come to be your very own personal yenta?"

"My what?"

"Yenta. What, you've never watched *Fiddler on the Roof*?"

"Guess not," I said. "What's a yenta?"

"A matchmaker. How come your boss has to set up dates for you?"

I paused. Thought about telling a lie, then decided against it. "I lost a bet. Actually several bets."

"He's making you do this?"

I nodded.

Darcy grinned, revealing a dimple in her left cheek. "God, he's such a liar. He told my mom you were shy and had a hard time talking to girls your own age. She bought his bullshit. By the time he finished his sad story of concern about your social life, my mom volunteered me to go out with you. He never even had to ask."

Laughing, I said, "He told me a different story. Said your mom caught you with some dude and was freaking out about it and now she wouldn't let you out of her sight. So the only way he could have any fun was to find someone else, someone your mom trusted, to get you out of the house for a few hours."

The smile slid from Darcy's face. "Wow, he told you the truth."

A few miles down the road she asked, "Is he paying you?"

"No. Not exactly. He made all kinds of offers, but I refused. No offense, but this is the last Saturday night of summer. And since I'm a senior, this is basically my last Saturday of my last real summer, so my first choice wasn't to spend it hanging out with some girl I'd never met."

When I glanced over at her, Darcy looked on the verge of tears. So I quickly added, "But that was when I figured there was something wrong with you. Had I known you were so pretty, I probably would've changed my mind."

Darcy Marie looked me up and down as if seeing me for the first time.

"And I thought you would be a total dweeb. Guess we were both wrong."

I wasn't certain, but it at least seemed that Darcy had just complimented me. At the very least, she'd labeled me as something other than a total dweeb.

"Bet your boyfriend is pissed your mom made you go out with me."

Darcy shook her head. "He's mad at me, too. We haven't talked in a few days. I think he went out of town to see his cousin's band play in Albuquerque. He was gonna take me, but that was before …"

"Before what?" I asked when she stopped talking.

"Before things went to shit. But I don't wanna talk about him, or my mom, or your jackass boss. Where are we going?"

"To eat, I guess. You hungry for anything in particular?"

She curled her lips. "God no. Just the idea of food makes me nauseous."

"A movie?"

Darcy shook her head. "Go ahead and kill me now. Just because they made us go on this date doesn't mean we have to be bored to death."

"So what do you want to do?"

She shrugged. "I don't know. What would you be doing right now if you weren't with me?"

"I'd be at the lake. Drinking beer and hanging out with my friends."

"Oh." The disappointment in her voice made it clear that idea was no better than the movies.

"How about you? What would you be doing?"

"My boyfriend, unless his roommates were home. Then we'd be drinking and listening to some tunes."

Now, I knew what Doyle would do if he were in my shoes. He'd chime in with some comment along the lines of … *How about I play the part of your boyfriend and let you do me*, but I wasn't nearly as brazen as Doyle. So I ignored the words *"doing"* and *"boyfriend"* and said, "I know a place that will sell me some beer, if you want."

"Beer is gross. I usually drink vodka, or wine coolers. Sometimes Boone's Farm."

"I think they have Boone's Farm, maybe even wine coolers."

"That's okay," she said. "I quit drinking."

"That's probably good," I said. "Your mom would freak if I brought you home smelling like booze, and I'm sure Doyle would give me a ration of shit if I ruined his grand scheme."

Darcy took her feet off the dash and turned to face me. "Like I care what either one of them thinks. It would serve her right for making me go out with someone she doesn't even know. She's such a fucking hypocrite. Says my boyfriend is too old. He's only nineteen. How old are you? Eighteen?"

"Seventeen. I don't turn eighteen until December."

"So? For all she knew you were some kind of serial rapist. Did she care? No. She was perfectly happy to send me off just so her and dickhead could crawl on top of each other without me hearing her moan and scream. Like I've never heard it before."

Pulling up at a stoplight, I looked over at Darcy. Her

eyes were moist and her bottom lip was quivering. For the second time in only ten minutes I thought she was going to cry. I didn't want that to happen, so I said, "Don't blame your mom. Remember, Doyle convinced her I was painfully shy and scared to even talk to girls my age."

Darcy sat there with her arms folded across her chest, staring blankly ahead.

As the light turned green, I continued trying to cheer her up. "For what it's worth, I'm no serial rapist. Grape Nuts, Lucky Charms, Wheaties. None of it turns me on."

Darcy looked over at me as if I'd lost my mind.

"Matter of fact, breakfast foods as a whole are not my thing. So you can also rule out me being an oatmeal, toast, or Pop-Tart rapist."

When Darcy smiled, I leaned closer and lowered my voice to a whisper, "Though if I'm being totally honest, bagels are kind of sexy. What with that hole in the middle and all."

She had a great laugh. A sort of giggle that reminded me of the tinkling of a wind chime. And she really was pretty. Even with congealed-blood-colored lips.

With a grin still on her face, Darcy leaned her head back and said, "I can't believe I am out on a Saturday night with a shit kicker."

"See there," I said. "Things are starting to look up. Already your wildest dreams are coming true."

"Why am I starting to think you're as big a bullshit artist as your boss?"

"Beats me, because I'm not even close. Doyle is in a bullshitting league of his own."

I drove on for several more minutes. Already I'd circled and backtracked over Amarillo's grid of major streets and still I had no idea where to take this girl. She didn't seem to mind, but I was getting sick of aimlessly driving around in Doyle's battered truck. And the heat was starting to get to me.

To this day I'm not sure why I pulled up to my high school's ag farm. The place had nothing even close to air conditioning, and even less to offer as far as entertainment, but as I unlocked the gate, Darcy never even questioned why we were there. The ag farm was bordered on the west by the city dog pound and the east by first a creek, then a newly-built golf course. Vacant lots lay to both the north and south. Since the golf course had yet to open and the dog pound had closed for the night, there was not another soul anywhere around. Maybe I wanted to show Darcy something I had built. Or at least had a hand in building. As we strolled the fenced-in closure, I pointed out the barn my class had constructed last year. I showed her places I'd welded and cinderblock walls I had constructed along with my classmates. A couple of feeder lambs and one Billy goat were the only animals that time of year. They followed us around, hoping I was there to feed them.

Eventually we wound up sitting in the open doorway of an old bob-tailed trailer, which served as the farm's grain storage shed. Without many animals to feed, the compartment was nearly empty, though the remnants of last year's straw and hay littered the splintered floor. With our feet dangling out the doorway, we sat and talked while staring out at the revolving sprinklers watering the fairways of the adjacent golf course. It was still a bit odd for me to see green grass and manicured trees where a cow pasture had stretched out only a few months before.

"God, it's hot," Darcy said. "We should go play in the sprinklers."

"Except that water is nasty," I said. "It comes from the sewage treatment plant up the road. They filter out the solid chunks, but that's about it. When the wind blows the other direction, you can smell it."

"Gross." Darcy crinkled her nose. "But I'm hot." And just like that she peeled off her Ramones t-shirt to reveal a lacy, electric blue bra.

I didn't want to stare, but damned if I could keep from it. Focusing hard on her face, I said, "You really are pretty."

Darcy grinned and said, "And you really are full of shit."

Then she kissed me. Or maybe I kissed her. Hell if I can say for certain. But there on the floor of that trailer, in the purplish light of dusk, with a girl I had only met a short time before, summer came to a spectacular end. In the years since that night I've heard tales of horrible and woeful first experiences, but I possess only fond memories of that evening I spent with Darcy Marie. I say evening and not night because the good times ended once we got dressed and headed back to the apartment she shared with her mom.

Dusk had given way to darkness by the time we left the ag farm. Perhaps that's why I didn't notice the straw in Darcy's hair, or the lipstick smeared on her cheek. Perhaps I was too drunk with euphoria to notice much of anything.

Darcy's mom, on the other hand, noticed everything. So did Doyle.

I'll give my boss credit. He not only noticed but led me out of the hostile situation faster than you can say "Navy Seal." Of course he yelled at me all the way back to his house.

"What the fuck, Travis? I didn't care if you had a little fun, but did you have to bring her back looking like she'd been gangbanged by a herd of goats! Couldn't you have at least pulled the damn hay out of her hair?"

"I never even noticed her hair."

"You damned sure noticed something about her! Didn't you?"

By the time we pulled into his gravel driveway, Doyle had relaxed. He finally laughed and said, "Hell, I'm actually kind of proud of you. I'll be cut off for at least a month, but at least we both had some fun tonight."

As it turned out, my escapade with Darcy was the end of Doyle and Delinda's relationship. No, she didn't end it because I slept with her daughter. Matter of fact, Delinda didn't end it at all. Doyle did.

As Doyle later told me, "I don't mind being a mother fucker, but a man's gotta draw a line somewhere, and no way do I wanna be a grandmother fucker."

So when Darcy Marie announced she was pregnant, Doyle decided to cut and run.

Chapter Thirteen

More Than I Bargained For

"Darcy's pregnant."

Those were the first words out of Doyle's mouth when I walked into work the following Monday.

The first school day of my senior year had been mediocre at best, but a screwed up class schedule and a shitty locker assignment were nothing compared to … *Hey, Travis, you know that gal you just recently soiled with a lifetime supply of sperm? She's in the family way and you are suspect numero uno.*

To be clear, Doyle merely said, "Darcy's pregnant," and nothing more. My mind, however, heard the much more sinister version. That same mind raced back in time some forty-two odd hours. To the instant inside that bob-tailed trailer when I realized the time, my time, had finally arrived.

"Wait," I'd whispered to Darcy. "I don't have anything. I mean, I do, but they're back in the glove box of my truck."

"It's okay." Darcy pulled me closer. "You don't need one. I'm on the pill."

Standing there in the middle of Pearl's Feed and Seed, I felt the full brunt of Doyle's blurted statement.

Darcy's pregnant.

I chastised myself for tossing common sense out the window. For taking the boss's truck, and leaving mine behind. For rendering worthless the nearly two-year-old package of just-in-case condoms stashed in my glove box. For believing Darcy and her sultry, "You don't need one. I'm on the pill." All of it formed a hurricane swirl of regret within me. My heart flailed away like a man tossed overboard. My head spun like balsa in a whirlpool. My very future capsized.

Then, in the same casual tone as he'd said, "Darcy's pregnant," Doyle tossed me a life preserver. "Turns out her and that boyfriend been doing more than dry hump on that couch," he said with a laugh.

It took me a few heartbeats to comprehend, but as the news sunk in, I took a deep, relieved breath. Only then did I realize what it all meant.

My first time was with a pregnant chick.

I'd tried to call Darcy on Sunday, the day after our date. Her mom had answered and told me it would be better if I didn't call back. Doyle's calls, however, had been accepted so he knew a few more details.

Apparently, Delinda had gone ape-shit crazy after Doyle and I made our hasty departure. Yelling and screaming, she ridiculed her daughter for taking chances with her body and doubly so for doing it with some boy she'd just met. But

Darcy trumped her by revealing that sleeping with me was hardly a risk, given the fact she was already pregnant and nearly two months along.

That's when Doyle told me he was ending it. Besides claiming to be too young to screw grandmas, he said, "Delinda will most likely end up raising the kid, and the last I want is to get mixed up taking care of a newborn.

"Best case scenario," he said, "is Darcy and her sperm donor get hitched. But even then Momma will wind up supporting them. And babysitting. And worrying about her daughter, her grandbaby, and God-only-knows what else. Women with that much shit on their mind are never any good in bed."

A few days later, the boss admitted he had his eye on another gal. "A professional woman, with a lot to offer."

By his tone alone, I knew when Doyle said "a lot to offer," he meant she had really big tits. When pressed, the boss revealed the identity of his new crush. His lawyer's legal secretary.

I'd met the secretary. She was indeed beautiful, but on her one visit to Pearl's Feed and Seed, she'd seemed anything but impressed by either my boss or the store. She'd dropped off some documents for Doyle to sign and scooted out the door *per valde festinatio*. That's "with great haste" for those not fluent in Latin, such as legal secretaries and fourth-year Latin students, like myself.

The legal secretary had entered the picture when Doyle's

bookie got popped in some sort of city-wide gambling sting. Turns out the name Doyle Suggs, along with the store's phone number, appeared regularly in the bookie's ledger.

Both Doyle and his lawyer, a man that could pass for Dennis Hopper's fashion-challenged twin brother, were trying to figure out a way to justify a not-guilty plea. The lawyer had a penchant for pastel suits and fedora-style hats, whereas Doyle wore denim overalls as often as not.

A gambler himself, Panama Jack the Lawyer often accompanied Doyle on out-of-town trips to the cockfights. I always wondered what other travelers thought when they saw the two of them together? But then again there was no telling what a person might see at the cockfights. I knew, because Doyle had taken me along a time or two as well.

You might think that legal scrutiny would deter the urge to wager, but Doyle wasn't about to let a little matter like the county D.A.'s office get in the way of his fun. A staunch believer in the old adage, *All work and no play makes Jack a dull boy,* Doyle made damn certain no one ever confused him for Jack. We played as much if not more than we worked, and at Pearl's the principles of play were the very same things that earned Vegas the name Sin City.

Gambling and sex. Sex and gambling. The order determined solely by Doyle's mood and bankroll. He liked to wager, yet two factors kept him from being a successful gambler. One, he often got too cocky. And two, he never knew when to quit. Those same attributes also described his love life. If

Doyle lost fifty bucks on one hand of poker, you could bet the house he was gonna wager a hundred the very next hand to try and regain what he'd lost. Chasing bad money with good. He did the exact same thing when it came to betting on football, baseball, or his very own invention, fly roulette.

Flies and the feed store went together like summer and ice cream. We fought the infestation, but our efforts were futile. Dozens of strips of sticky fly paper hung in various locations around the store, and fly sprayers squirted insecticide at timed intervals, but Doyle's big gun was a giant-ass bug zapper that hung up front.

That bug zapper and its bluish neon light mesmerized Doyle. He could pretty much tell you what kind of insect just got fried by the tone and length of the sizzle. He would sit up front, sipping his coffee, and watching the contraption, waiting for some unsuspecting critter to meet its maker. He developed an entire philosophical theory about the bug zapper, equating it to the light humans who've had a near-death experience often describe. He wouldn't go so far as to say God had a giant bug zapper that served as the gateway to heaven, but Doyle definitely believed there was a correlation. Though he struggled to answer why bugs that saw the light never came back to life the way so many humans claim to have done.

Given the boss's fascination, I was not surprised when he invented fly roulette. Doyle was looking for a game that several people could play at once, but he also wanted to bump up the house odds to make an extra buck or ten. So, he fashioned a piece of plywood about a yard square and painted numbers in two-inch squares. He then positioned the board under the bug zapper. The idea was for the gambler to choose one of the squares and lay down money that the next fried insect carcass would land within the confines of their chosen number.

The ill-fated game was fraught with problems from the very beginning. Flies usually stayed intact and generally landed in one piece, but moths fragmented and often landed in multiple squares. Sometimes a bug hung in the grate, only to be dislodged by the next flying critter falling from the zapper. Determining which fell first was no easy chore. Realizing fly roulette was riddled with too many inconsistencies, Doyle had no choice but to abandon his invention.

That left poker as the game of choice whenever a sizable group of five or more loitered about the store. Doyle's knack for reading people made him a solid player, but more than once his cockiness erased an hour's worth of winnings in a single hand.

If it happened to be only the two of us, Doyle and I sometimes pitched quarters. But it was a game the boss easily grew bored with. Or so he claimed. Ask me, and I'll tell you he hated to pitch quarters because I won more times than not. Had the stakes been higher than twenty-five cents a throw, I doubt we'd have played at all.

Regardless of the game, Doyle didn't take well to losing.

Neither did he like being thwarted when it came to carnal pursuits of the flesh. Which is exactly why he was determined to win over the legal secretary.

Rose was her name, and maybe it was her beauty or perhaps it was merely the challenge, but for whatever reason, she became Doyle's obsession. Like a migrating salmon, Doyle refused to be denied. Dam the stream. Pollute the waters. Threaten him with a hungry grizzly. And still Doyle swam along, fighting the current, risking death in order to spawn.

I, on the other hand, fresh from my near-hooking, now recognized just how deadly the waters could be. Samantha Blake and I did not share a single class my senior year, so my fixation for the cheerleader withered on the vine. Candy Bailloux had departed for sunny Florida, and sadly, I didn't know any other girls who frequently gave blowjobs out in the feed shed. My solitary encounter with Darcy Marie had left me with a fond memory and a congealed blood-colored stain on my best shirt, but she too was gone from my life.

There were plenty of other girls at my school, but it seemed like half of them were pregnant and the other half already had boyfriends. Which was just as well, given the fact my near miss had me quite spooked of the opposite sex. It wasn't the girls I feared as much as myself. The fact so many of my classmates already had a kid, or one on the way, brought home just how easy it was to conceive a child. Like most teenagers, I wasn't intelligent enough to realize

I was still a kid myself. However, I did posses ample savvy to know getting some gal pregnant would be the death of most, if not all, of my goals.

Until that night with Darcy, I'd considered my peers both reckless and stupid. I understood the desire to copulate. What adolescent boy in the throes of puberty doesn't? But only a fool would forgo a condom. Or so I'd always said.

One assurance from a girl I barely knew, and I'd turned into just such a fool. Sure, I'd gotten lucky, in more ways than one. But the experience had left me shaken. What if Darcy had lied? What if she were one of those girls looking for a way out? A way to escape her mom's rules?

I didn't want to become a dad at seventeen, eighteen, or anytime in the foreseeable future. But Darcy had exposed me, again in more ways than one. I was a hypocrite. I'd passed judgment on so many of my classmates, and yet I had lacked the willpower to apply the brakes on my runaway lust. What if it happened again?

I suppose in my mind I thought, *One girl was willing to have sex with me, so no doubt hoards of others will soon follow suit.* I suppose I imagined girls calling me at all hours and crawling through my bedroom window to keep me warm at night. I suppose I was delusional. But after the scare with Darcy, I made myself a promise to not have sex with, to not date, to not so much as cast a wanton look at a single member of the opposite sex until I graduated high school.

There are some objectives that a pubescent seventeen-year-old boy simply cannot achieve, so I of course failed to maintain my lofty hike down the high road. However, I wasn't alone in my failures. Doyle had set his sight and his heart on Rose, but as the months ticked by, the legal secretary continued to shun my boss. He called, hand-delivered her lunch, even stooped to sending her florist-bought flowers.

None of it impressed Rose.

Sometime around Christmas, Doyle's bookie pled guilty to a lesser charge than illegal bookmaking. The plea eroded the state of Texas's case against Doyle and all the other names gleaned from the bookie's ledger, but the boss didn't let that deter him. He continued his pursuit despite Rose's reticence and the clearing of his good name.

To be fair to my boss, I should point out that the only reason my name did not appear in the bookie's ledger was because Doyle placed my wagers for me. In reality, I was every bit the gambler he was. Maybe more so, since I often possessed unrealistic visions of hitting the big payoff. I teetered on the very edge of addiction, whereas Doyle wagered more for the thrill and excitement.

Doyle and I bet sports regularly. Football especially. Parlays, over/unders, money lines, juice. I learned the meaning of these terms while working at Pearl's. Despite the fact my paychecks barely topped a hundred bucks during the school year, it was nothing for me to wager five or six hundred dollars over a football weekend. I won some, lost some, but always managed to stay close enough to pay my debt on the weeks I missed more games than I hit.

But my biggest gamble that year did not come in the form of a sports wager, nor did it occur within the confines of Pearl's Feed and Seed.

Armed with letters of recommendation from my FFA teacher and from Doyle's dad, Buck, the actual owner of Pearl's, I walked right inside Amarillo National Bank and headed to the loan department. I presented my case to the loan officer only to be told I needed to head upstairs to the fifth floor, since they had an entire department devoted to agricultural endeavors.

Without an appointment, I sat out near the secretary's desk for a good half-hour. Between phone calls, the woman behind the big mahogany desk asked me questions, which I politely answered.

"No, thank you. I'm not thirsty."

"Yes, I did talk to them downstairs before coming up here."

"No, I did not bring a parent with me."

A good many of Doyle's lessons had taken root in my mind by that time, so I hadn't even thought to be nervous.

All they can say is no.

Never hurts to ask.

You can't hear yes until you got the balls to ask.

Those ideals had brought me to the bank, but thanks to the woman's barrage of questions, those self-assurances eroded like a turd in a thunderstorm. Each time I answered, the secretary's left brow arched a little higher.

Sitting there, I again ran the numbers through my head. Three show pigs, which would cost at least five hundred apiece. Double that, if the auction got crazy. A lamb with a decent pedigree would be another four or five hundred. Feed, medicine, straw for bedding and other supplies would add another six, maybe seven hundred to the overall tally. That meant I needed to borrow at least three grand to properly fund my final year in FFA. And a bank loan was the only way I was gonna have the cash to make it happen.

So what if I was a high school kid with a part-time, minimum wage job.

So what if I had absolutely zero credit established.

So what if the snooty secretary was now unable to hide her smirk.

After a good, long lapse, the call came. I could go back. The man had a corner office with a great view of the city courthouse lawn. His desk was twice the size of his secretary's, and after shaking his hand I sat in the largest, comfiest leather chair my butt ever had the pleasure of occupying.

The man looked me right in the eye and said, "What can I do for you today?"

I laid it out there. I told him my plans, my goal, my strategy for raising the animals and competing not only locally, but at the big stock shows downstate. He listened carefully. He intently studied the recommendation letters. He scrutinized me as I spoke. I could tell my being there was somewhat of an oddity. No doubt the man was used to extending loans for hundreds of thousands of dollars. His normal clients were ranchers, wheat farmers, and other assorted land buyers. Not seventeen-year-old boys with nothing more than hope and want-to to serve as collateral.

Finally the bank officer said, "Three hogs and a lamb. Is three thousand enough to purchase four animals and feed them for the year?"

"Yes, sir," I replied. "Actually, I only have to feed them until the February shows in San Antonio and Houston."

"I've been doing farm and ranch loans for two decades," the man said. "But you're the first FFA student to ever sit at my desk. Now I'm wondering why that is." The man leaned back and scratched his chin before saying, "Tell you what, I'm gonna give you four-thousand at our lowest rate. We'll schedule a single payment due in May. That should give you plenty of time to get your checks in when you sell your stock at those February shows."

Twenty minutes later I walked out with a huge smile on my face, a deposit slip on a brand new account, and a confident, almost-cocky attitude. The money would buy me some top notch pigs and a hell of show lamb. I didn't have a shred of doubt that I would double the four grand in the show ring.

Never did I consider the fact four grand was pretty much equal to every last dollar I would take home from Pearl's between then and the time the loan was due. Never did I think about starting a savings account to squirrel away part of my paychecks. Never did I ponder what would happen if I didn't have the cash to pay back that loan.

Chapter Fourteen

Better Lucky Than Good

After spending nearly twenty-six hundred dollars on a trio of well-bred piglets and one robust young lamb, I still felt quite good about myself. My mood didn't change until castration day arrived.

Every kid who bought a show animal was supposed to castrate his or her own critter. The lambs were easy. Removing their gonads was as simple as placing a tight rubber band-like ring around the scrotum. The band cut the blood flow off until the entire sack turned black and rotted away. Lopping the nuts off a pig was a wee bit more intense.

We boys squirmed at the idea of the lambs slow-to-go family jewels, but the lack of blood rendered the event stomachable for most. The majority of my classmates did not deal as well with catching a squealing, squirming piglet, holding it upside down, slicing open its scrotum, and cutting out the enclosed testicles.

I was not part of the majority.

Having been raised in a family that butchered its own meat, I knew beef, chicken, and pork did not originate from cellophane-wrapped packages at the back of the grocery store. Nut-cutting was (and is) a dirty but delicate task that had to be performed if you wanted to show your animal. Only a handful of us in the class had the stomach and skill to do the deed, and I don't mean to brag, but I was the most adept among them. So, that year I had a direct hand in de-balling something in the neighborhood of seventy-five pigs. To be technically correct, I should call them barrows from this point on, as that is the proper term for a castrated pig.

Out of those seventy-five freshly created barrows, only one had a problem. My nearly nine-hundred dollar, black and white Hampshire. The day after separating the ill-fated porker from his prized possessions, I arrived at the school farm. Yes, the very same place where my own chicherones had intimately been introduced to Darcy. And what did I find when I arrived at the farm? My pig, my barrow, my investment. Dead, departed, deceased. Stiffer than a bulldog's dick. (Perhaps you need to reread chapter one if you've forgotten just how proficient a bulldog's apparatus is.)

Losing a quarter of my investment hurt, but when the school's entire herd of pigs got sick two weeks later, I was scared absolutely shitless. Of course, I was the only thing at the ag farm shitless, as the collection of barrows were anything but.

Some sort of intestinal bug had the whole bunch defecating in explosive fashion. A dozen or so died, and right about then I was wishing pig shit could be barreled and sold like crude oil. Because unless something changed, and soon, runny pig shit would be the only green currency I'd have to repay that bank loan.

    I spent hours at the farm doctoring the sick animals. Not just mine, but everybody's. Every daylight hour I wasn't at school, or at Pearl's, I spent giving shots, changing tainted water, or shoveling dirty shit.

    The swine eventually kicked their case of the scours, but every last one of them was undersized and had failed to put on enough pounds. Would they catch up in time to make the qualifying weight for the county show in January? Our ag teacher seemed skeptical, but I had no choice. If I was gonna repay that loan, my pigs had to be shown.

    Again, I spent countless hours at the farm, almost force feeding the hogs. When not attending the barrows, I exercised my lamb so he would put on extra muscle tone.

    My worry about the loan grew, when thanks to all the extra medicine and the special, protein-enhanced feed I'd been buying, I blew through the rest of my borrowed money a good month before the county show.

    During cold snaps, I climbed out of my nice warm bed an hour early to go bust ice out of the tanks and provide fresh water for the pigs. When it snowed, I shoveled the drifts so my porkers wouldn't burn excess calories. And always, rain or shine, warm or cold, my boots, my truck, and yes, even myself, carried the unmistakable whiff of swine dung. That fact alone made my no-dating embargo easier to maintain as that particular stench is known to keep wolves, vampires, and teenage girls at bay.

The last weekend in January was cold, windy, and icy, but it felt like paradise to me when both of my surviving barrows, a cross-bred and a Berkshire, made weight and qualified for the Potter County Junior Livestock Show. Many of the pigs from our school were not so lucky.

My relief, however, was short-lived when my two swine each finished a disappointing third in their class. That qualified them for the sale, but just barely. And the lamb that I'd been taking for long, three-mile walks and heart-attack inducing sprints for better than four months? It came in second to last, meaning it wouldn't earn squat at the local show.

For the uneducated, let me tell you about a county livestock show. The exhibitors enter, hoping to make the sale, but sale is technically the wrong word, as none of the animals change ownership. The funds are more like donations, in that the 4-H and FFA competitors get to keep their animal and show them again. The so-called "buyers" write off their expenditures come tax time.

The bigger livestock shows work somewhat differently. There, every animal entered meets the same fate: The meat market, where they get butchered to eventually be served up to hungry carnivores. Those that place also make a sale where rich donors bid for the right to pay outlandish prices for a pig, lamb, or steer. Again these "buyers" do not get to keep or even sample the meaty goodness. They do get one hell of a tax break, because at these shows, the grand champions can fetch better than six figures at auction.

Regardless of how well the animal placed, every competitor gets a check for the meat market value of their entry, but market prices would not come anywhere near covering my four-grand loan.

Neither would the six-hundred and twenty-five dollars I received in the county auction.

Still, thirty-four-hundred in the hole, I headed to San Antonio, Texas, in early February of 1991, fearing my gamble had indeed been a sucker bet and feeling as embittered as I had that day at Pearl's when Doyle beat me first at blackjack, then poker, then dice, until I was so far behind I had no choice but to succumb and take his girlfriend's daughter out on a date. To this day I am certain he somehow scammed me, but I couldn't prove it then, and I can't prove it now. Though in the end, the screwing I took turned out to be far better than I ever imagined.

In San Antonio, my confidence soared when ag teacher after ag teacher stopped by and commented on my crossbred.

"He's a good one."

"Ought make the sale for sure."

"Hell of a hog."

I grinned and said thanks at every comment, but the year had taught me fate was full of surprises that could shrivel up a person's confidence faster than pig skin in a deep fryer.

I was hopeful, but refused to count my pork rinds before they were fried.

The first step at the bigger shows is to make the actual show ring and not be sent straight to the meat truck. A judge takes one gander at each animal and either lets it pass on, or he sends it straight down a walkway where a ramp leads to a large semi-trailer. The ramp meant your animal was bound direct for the slaughter house. The ramp meant market price. Maybe two-hundred-and-fifty dollars, if you were lucky.

Avoiding the ramp, me and my cross-bred made it to the show ring. Maybe it was my nerves. Maybe my pig was simply feeling frisky, but the second we hit that enclosure things went to hell.

The idea was to slowly walk your barrow by the judge. Let him see the animal's strengths while hiding its weaknesses. Say your pig is pinched in the ass-end, but looks great head on. That meant you, as a shower, were expected to give the judge multiple looks head on. Once by the judge, it was in your best interest to step between and obstruct his view of the subpar hams. All without looking obvious about your intentions.

My cross-bred had few weaknesses according to those who knew, so my assignment was to give the judge good long-looks early and often. But my barrow hit the ring and suddenly transformed into Seattle Slew. He ran around the perimeter like Carl Lewis at the Coliseum. I trailed behind trying to rein him in, but the ring was full of kids and other barrows. Ag teachers and 4-H leaders rimmed the enclosure and barked out orders to their pupils.

"Slow him the hell down," my teacher urged with every lap.

The pig did finally stop, to bite a chunk out of some other hog's ear. Men with large wooden planks stepped in to break up the swine soiree, and then before I could even think, the judge pointed to my barrow and said something. The men then herded me out of the ring.

I was out. Me and my pig had failed. I exited the runway, and Swineatariat waddled up the gangplank on his way to becoming next week's sausage McMuffin.

As I watched my animal disappear among a sea of other pigs, my ag teacher slung an arm over my shoulder. "Well, you made it to the sale, but just barely."

He was disappointed, I was disappointed. The barrow was good enough to place much higher, but I'd failed to show it well enough to prove that point. On the upside, I was only the second student from Caprock High School to ever make the sale at San Antonio. A few years before, a kid had placed fourth in his class and received fourteen hundred dollars in the auction. I, on the other hand, had just come in twelfth. Simple math told me whatever I received was going to be well short of what I needed to pay off my loan. That meant I would have only the Houston Livestock Show and Rodeo in which to bail my butt out of a jam. I would have to wait three weeks for that show, but at least I had both a lamb and a barrow entered at Houston. Two chances were better than one, but first I had to see what my barrow brought at the San Antonio auction.

As the auctioneer got things started, I hoped to make at least a thousand toward my loan. The grand champion barrow sold for nearly forty-thousand dollars. The reserve champion went for half that. The breed champions came next. They all fetched right around five grand. After that, the premiums began dropping fast. It was a long time before my turn came, as my pig was scheduled to be the very last one in the sale. I only hoped all those rich people still had money left by then.

Standing on the sidelines, I watched the wealthy donors put away barrels of booze. As they spent their money, the men in tuxedos and women in evening gowns mostly ignored the kids and animals up on the stage. They glanced that way only long enough to raise their hand and bid, but for the most part they shook each other's hands, slapped each other's backs, and mingled as if at a cocktail party. They resembled politicians seeking re-election. Later, I discovered some of them actually were.

The hours ticked along, with the auctioneer constantly goading one bidder or another, reminding them why they were gathered. When my turn neared, I gathered in the back alongside a pig that was not my own. My barrow had already departed the premises in the back of a semi, but the show officials held back several animals of each breed so that we could parade out to the auction ring with an animal in tow.

Not that it really mattered at that point. Most of the buyers had consumed enough liquor that they wouldn't have noticed had I been riding an emu named Englebert.

Standing and waiting with only three or four kids left before me, I hoped for the best. I'd been watching the numbers closely, and while the majority of exhibitors were getting right around nine hundred or a grand for their animals, occasionally someone got twice that. There seemed to be no rhyme or reason as to why or when a sudden spike would occur.

When there were just two of us left, me and a freshman girl from a tiny town down near the Gulf, the man in charge looked at us and said, "Y'all are the lucky ones. Especially you." He pointed to me.

"Why am I lucky?" I asked as the girl headed out.

"You'll see. Last pig in the auction always fetches a ton. Those people all came here to donate some money. You will be their last chance to spend it."

"Sold, for twenty-two-hundred dollars," came the auctioneer's booming voice. The freshman's hog fetched more than any in the last hour.

"Your turn," the man said to me. "Don't forget to smile when you get out there."

My heart fluttered as I stepped out into the bright lights. The pig I'd been assigned was content to stick his head in a slop bucket and eat, so there was no need for me to do anything, but stand there and smile. It felt awkward as hell, but the fake grin didn't last long. I couldn't actually see out into the audience, thanks to the glare.

"Folks, this is it. The very last barrow in the 1991 San Antonio Livestock Show and Rodeo. Who'll start me out? Give me Fi- fi-five hundred."

The number climbed rapidly. Five-hundred, nine-hundred, two grand. Three, four, and sold!

"For fifty-seven hundred dollars!"

I was shocked. Stunned. But one thing was for certain. The fake smile on my face was gone, replaced by a very genuine, shit-eating grin.

My pig had just earned more than all the other barrows except for the grand and reserve champion. I was taking home more prize money by finishing twelfth and being the final pig in the sale, than I would have had I won breed champion. Like Doyle always said, "It's better to be lucky than good." Months of worry erased in a single instant. Standing there, all that hard work and lost sleep seemed not like a sacrifice, but a privilege.

Step two in the process was to pose for a picture with the buyer. Normally it was a quick forty-five second deal. Step in front of a curtain bearing the show's name and logo, smile and shake the donor's hand while the bulbs flashed. A quick thank you later and everyone goes their separate ways.

That's how it is supposed to go. My photo shoot did not.

For one thing, everyone was exiting the area as I stepped out. For another, the man who'd just spent nearly six grand on me and my barrow knew every single person who walked by. With a high ball glass full of amber liquid in his left hand, he shook dozens of others with his right. The photographer tried to corral him for a shot, but he couldn't be pinned down.

I guessed the man to be in his late sixties, but nearly everyone stopped to talk to him. Young, old. Male, female. Didn't matter. Without fail, my buyer and his friends would cut-up laughing, despite the obvious irritation of the photographer. Finally the buyer grew tired of the photographer's interruptions and said, "Hell, that boy doesn't want a picture with a crusty old man like me anyway." He snapped his fingers. "Bambi! Candi! Come over here and pose for a picture with this boy."

Two of the world's most gorgeous women stepped forward. I'm talking *Playboy* model beautiful. Both brunettes, one in a skin-tight shimmering blue evening gown, the other wearing an almost see-through white dress. Both outfits offered enough cleavage to render an adolescent boy like myself speechless, as the girls, actually women, stepped up beside me.

"Good," the photographer said. "Now lean forward and rest a hand on your animal."

I did what I was told. The pig that wasn't really mine still had his nose in the feed bucket anyway.

"Girls, scoot in. You," the photographer pointed at me, "look up."

I did and bam, the flash went off. There I am in the picture, a red-faced boy without a care in the world. A boob on my left cheek, a boob on my right cheek. My broad grin spanning the distance in-between. As the photographer packed up his things, the buyer stepped over to me. I thanked him, and we shook hands. Then he offered me a bit of advice.

"Son, invest your money wisely," he said gathering in his two dates. "And one of these days, you'll be able to afford a pair of these." Then, with a squeeze of each girl's ass, he staggered away with a smile matched only by my own.

Chapter Fifteen

Two Turtle Doves

I consider two to be my lucky number. Why, you ask? Boobs came in sets of two. They're good. I've won a fair amount of money shooting dice over the years. Craps is played with a pair of bones. Then there's Noah, who, under God's guidance, repopulated the world by the grace of two-by-two. But if I'm honest, my reasons are more selfish and flakier than those listed above. To this day I have a proliferation of twos in my life, but follow along as I tell you how the number became transfixed in my consciousness.

The man who bought my pig at San Antonio turned out to be the heir of a nationally known retail store. I of course can't tell you his name, due to the delicate nature of his marital status and the fact neither Candi nor Bambi shared his last name. But I will say, right there at the end of his last name was the Roman Numeral II. Had the man been worth less than seven figures, no doubt he would've simply gone by So-and-So Junior, but being filthy rich made him So-and So the *second*.

Two weeks after So-and-So the *second* bailed me out of

my financial quandary; I headed to Houston, Texas, with my second surviving barrow, a fine looking black and white Berkshire. Long story short, I kicked ass. The pig cooperated, I showed like I'd never showed before, and when all was said and done, my animal was declared Breed Champion. Houston paid even better than San Antonio, so at the auction sale I received fourteen-thousand-two hundred dollars for my prized porker. A *pair* of donors teamed together on the bid. They were neither famous, nor drunk, nor adorned with the eye-candy So-and-So the second had been. Nevertheless, I was a damned happy eighteen-year-old.

My lamb failed to place but the two meat market checks for my animals added with the auction funds of my barrow totaled better than fifteen grand, and after San Antonio I didn't owe anybody a single dime. The cash was all mine.

My goal had been to double the four grand I borrowed, but I turned that four grand into a whopping sum of—wait for it—*Twenty-two* thousand-*two* hundred dollars and *two* cents. That's four more twos for those keeping score.

With the cash I bought an acre of land, which I still own, a used pickup that served me well until a carload of illegal aliens smacked me head on, and I fully funded my first year of college. Sadly, I'm not sure the winnings would be enough pay for even one of those things in today's economy, but at the time it was a near fortune to a guy who made $3.25 an hour at the feed store.

The trend of twos didn't exist solely within my agriculture

endeavors. My social structure fell in the same category. For the duration of my senior year, I had *two* best friends—both female. I still had my guy buddies, Scott, Jason, Brent, but the latter was married with a kid and the others had steady girlfriends, who dominated their spare time.

    I became Duckie, from Pretty in Pink, and Anthony Michael Hall from every movie he was ever in. A guy. A friend. The very thing no male ever wants to be. The dreaded "guyfriend,"—a totally platonic buddy for girls to confide in and unload every bit of angst and anger onto for the wrongs done unto them by their real boyfriend. I never planned to be one of those guys. Nevertheless, it happened. Twice.

    Sherry came first. You may remember her as the girl I got to know while playing matchmaker for the cue ball flinging Cody Hawkins.

    Senior year, Sherry and I shared the exact same schedule. Despite the fact she was better than five months pregnant, Sherry wasn't showing when school started. Her boyfriend, Curtis, had graduated the year before, so given the fact we walked to and from every class together, half the school assumed the baby was mine once her belly began to swell.

    Sherry was a beautiful girl, so I found the rumors flattering. Being that she was a very pretty girl and I was a horny teenage boy in the throes of puberty, I had pondered the possibilities, but not in any desperate or long-ranging way.

    I understood we were meant to be pals and nothing more. Besides, she loved Curtis, and despite my initial thoughts of the dude, he too eventually turned into one of my best friends in the world.

At about the eight month mark, Sherry became homebound due to complications in her pregnancy. I visited nearly every day and hauled homework back and forth for her, which I suppose is what mislead Mrs. Brazille.

Mrs. Brazille taught senior English and, perhaps a week after Sherry left school, she asked me to hang after class. I assumed she was going to chastise me for the third-rate essay over *Canterbury Tales* I'd turned in the day before. Even back then I was an avid reader, but Chaucer's magnum opus made me long for a .44 magnum. I felt certain the book was better suited to be a target than a source of intellectual enlightenment, so I'd finally given up and resorted to CliffsNotes and a three page paper of pure opius bullshit.

As my classmates filed into the hall, Mrs. Brazille stood before me, her arms folded across her chest. No easy task given the fact my English teacher had ginormous boobs of a bizarre conical shape. Madonna had yet to make the look popular.

"Young man, what are your plans for the future?"

"Huh?"

"Upon graduation. Surely you have some type of plan?"

Her tone strongly suggested she was put out with me, though she'd yet to mention *Canterbury Tales*.

"I'm going to school, I guess. Probably just Amarillo College."

"College is fine and dandy," Mrs. Brazille snapped. "But you have more than your own future to consider, Mister."

I was still trying to digest the angry righteousness behind the way she'd said "Mister," when Mrs. Brazille asked, "Will you be getting married?"

"Married?" I shot her a confused look. "I can't imagine why I would."

Spittle actually flew from the teacher's mouth as she launched into a nearly incomprehensible tirade about ... *boys like me ... who have your fun and move on ... leaving innocent girls, like Sherry, to bear the burden alone.*

Catching the underlying direction of the inquisition I tried to explain I was not the father. That Sherry and I were merely friends, but Mrs. Brazille heard only what she wanted. She took my words as but more excuses to shirk my duties. I passed her class with an A, though to this day I'm certain it pained her to give me such a grade, as never again that semester did the woman smile my way.

I truly hope that someday Mrs. Brazille picks up a copy of *The Feedstore Chronicles* and, while overlooking my misplaced commas and questionable grammar, realizes her mistake.

Actually, I've seen my old English teacher twice since graduation. In a cruel twist of fate, I was alone on two separate occasions with Sherry and Carly, her daughter with Curtis. Carly was but a few months old on the first occurrence, and not more than a year or so old the second. No doubt seeing us together only reinforced our English teacher's erroneous assertion that my dangling participles were the root of the problem.

Curtis and Sherry have been married right at twenty years now, and they have four lovely daughters every bit as beautiful as their mother. I'm proud to still call them friends.

Wendy Cole. That was the name of my other best friend. Having grown up right around the corner from each other, Wendy and I had always known each other and been friends to a certain extent. But that senior year we were together far more than we'd ever been. All those mornings I got up early to trudge to the ag farm, in the rain, in the snow, and in the freezing cold face of winter's frigid north winds, Wendy was right there beside me. We rode to school together. We ate lunch together. We hung out together. Like Sherry, Wendy too had a boyfriend. But he went to another school so I rarely saw the dude. We were not friends in any sense of the word. All facts that made it easier for me to wish he would disappear and open a door for me.

I liked Wendy as a friend, but I'd be lying if I didn't admit hanging out with her that much also brought into focus her other assets. And when I say assets, I might as well start with the first three letters of the word. No one, not even Candy Bailloux, had ever filled out a pair of Rocky Mountain jeans the way Wendy did. She had blonde locks, captivating pale blue eyes, and a curvy figure overshadowed only by her vivacious spirit.

Wendy had it all, and she was a lot of fun to hang out with. I didn't know any other girls like her. She wasn't afraid to get pig shit on her boots, or chug a beer, but rest assured she was no tomboy.

Wendy Cole added a sex appeal to whatever she was doing. And she put up with my goofiness like few others could. She smoked, but never smelled like an ashtray. To help cover the smell, she kept a little squirt bottle of coconut air freshener in her car. One day, while playing with her cigarette lighter I decided to see if the spray was flammable.

It was.

The resulting fireball was quite impressive, and while Wendy yelled at me profusely, she got over her anger long before her right eyebrow grew back.

So when Doyle decided to hire springtime help, to take care of the flowers in the greenhouse and run the register when we got busy, I rushed to recommend Wendy for the job. Doyle listened to my affirmations and, of course, saw right through them.

"Let me guess," The boss said. "You're not screwing this gal. But want to."

"It's not that," I lied. "She needs a job. You wanna hire someone. Seems like a perfect fit to me."

"Is she hot?"

"Yeah," I answered. "She is."

"Big tits?"

"Not especially, but she has a great ass."

Doyle chewed the corner of his recently grown mustache. "Is she legal?"

"Legal?"

"Eighteen," the boss said. "I might decide to beat you to the punch and have some fun myself, but I don't wanna go to jail."

"She has a boyfriend."

"So? I'm not a puss like you. I ain't afraid to break a few rules."

Doyle hired her and while I'm fairly certain the boss never had the brand of fun with Wendy he'd imagined, that did not stop him from trying to convince me otherwise.

Doyle took her to lunch. Often. Nearly daily to be exact, and they stayed gone long beyond the time required to eat. Many afternoons he invited her to his office "to see something," only to keep her back there long enough for my imagination to "see" all kinds of things. And he, of course, dropped innuendos at every opportunity. All of it together pissed me off. I had no claim to Wendy or her time, but his toying with her just to bother me peeved me far beyond anything else he'd ever done. Doyle had been irritating me for years by that point, but not warning me about a bulldog getting jacked off, and forcing me to think Doyle had become the bulldog, were two different types of emotion.

Wendy assured me he only did those things to make me mad. I didn't doubt her, but in the past Doyle's behavior had seemed more about entertaining himself and having a good time, less about pissing on my leg. Wendy was a smart girl. I hoped she wasn't buying his bullshit, but I'd seen him fool a lot of women.

Anger. Jealousy. Fear. Call it what you want, but I couldn't stand the sensations any longer. I became an asshole of epic proportions. I could never change Doyle, but I could drive Wendy away. I encouraged, in fact, pushed her to quit and, eventually, she did just that.

My behavior eroded our friendship and after graduation we drifted apart. Pregnant with her boyfriend's son, she married the dude that fall, and while I never got to know the guy, he proved to be the one true, perfect match for Wendy. They've been married for better than two decades and have two strapping boys of their own. We do not live in the same town, but thanks to Facebook, Wendy and I now keep up with each other's lives.

I am appreciative of her forgiving nature, since the very act of forgiveness is granting a second chance. Second, as in the number two, and if working for and around Doyle spawned anything, it was the need for second chances.

Chapter Sixteen

It Wasn't B'aaaad

Wendy's departure meant that, once again, it was just Doyle and me. Maybe it was the fact I'd graduated high school and was forced to think about the future. Or perhaps, I simply had not forgiven Doyle for the way things turned out with Wendy, but it was that summer that I saw the darker side to Doyle.

Three ruined marriages, even if the last two were to the same woman. A woman who felt compelled to try and kill him. Twice. All of his relationships, even the platonic ones, had come to an abrupt end. Hopalong was six feet under. Jimmy Bluejacket was sitting in prison. Tasha had never been seen since her pesticide flinging breakdown. A string of others girlfriends had sworn Doyle off. Most would rather see him dead than alive, and I bore witness to them all. I wondered if it was possible to have any type of connection with Doyle and not be subjected to tragedy. No story brings this point home quite like the tale of Doyle and Ginger's friendship, and the demise thereof.

As described elsewhere in this book, Ginger was one of

our more normal patrons. More normal, of course, being relevant to the comparison group. Nowhere, outside of Pearl's, would a middle-aged woman with an unhealthy infatuation with a goat named Wagner be considered normal.

Once upon a time Ginger had been married. Doyle told me her inability to conceive children led to her divorce, so I used my own amateur psychology skills to deduce that Wagner had filled the void left by Ginger's barren womb. Ginger was an intelligent woman, an avid reader like me, and an accomplished artist. I enjoyed talking to her, but over time, it became apparent she was also a lonely, depressed woman in need of human contact.

"You should take her out sometime," I told Doyle. "Make her happy. Heck, I'll even babysit Wagner so y'all can be alone."

Doyle answered with, "Been there, done that."

I was shocked. Not that he'd bedded yet another woman, but that he'd kept it a secret. Doyle wasn't one to keep his conquests quiet, and yet I'd never heard this story.

"And?"

"Wasn't baaahaaad." He grinned after his poorly done goat imitation.

"I'm serious," I said.

"So am I," Doyle replied. "I've had all of goat woman I care to."

Several months went by and it became all the more evident Ginger had problems. She would come in with her hair a ratted mess, and her clothes wrinkled and stained with paint. Rather than pay with cash, she began charging the items she purchased.

Despite the decline of her own appearance, Wagner's fur was as bright and shiny as ever. By this time he was a full-sized goat with a long, six-inch goatee and shiny horns of approximately the same length. On a leash, he still accompanied her everywhere she went.

Ginger's account grew each month until finally, Doyle told her he couldn't let her charge unless she paid some of the bill down. Ginger cried and left. We didn't see her for several months.

Then came the day she walked in, with Wagner on his leash and a big plastic tub full of combs, baby shampoo, swaddling blankets, and other assorted crap she considered essential in the care of her beloved goat. I snickered while she begged Doyle to watch over her baby so she could fly to Vermont to be with her great aunt, who wasn't expected to live more than a few days.

Doyle never would've said yes, except Ginger owed him better than five-hundred dollars at the time. Assuring him this particular aunt was loaded, Ginger claimed to be the sole heir. Once the aunt croaked, she would settle the estate and be back to pay Doyle every last penny she owed, plus some, to cover the cost of Wagner's care.

Wagner had spent his days living in Ginger's spare room, where he had a bed, a TV, and more creature comforts than any goat should be afforded. At Pearl's, he found himself outside, in a fifteen-by-twenty foot dirt enclosure littered with chicken shit, rocks, and broken shingles from our dilapidated roof.

And Wagner didn't like it.

Not one damned bit.

Maybe he missed his nightly dose of Golden Girls reruns, or his daily brushing, or his frequent bubble baths. I can't really say what set him off, but Wagner soon figured out how to use those horns. The second you turned your back—WHAM! He head-butted you with enough force to lift you off your feet. Doyle found the goat's aggression quite humorous. Then again, he never ventured into the pen. I was the one who took care of the animals.

One week went by.

Then two.

Three.

Four.

Doyle called the phone number Ginger had left. Several times, but never got an answer.

"That's what you get," I teased Doyle. "You had your fun with Ginger and now it's your turn to raise y'all's lovechild." I spent the next several weeks bleeting out, "Daaa … dee," every chance I got. Like Doyle's human kids, Wagner proved to be a destructive hoodlum.

It was a Monday morning when Wagner finally made his biggest and last mistake. Actually, Monday morning was when we discovered the damage. Sometime over the weekend, the goat had chewed a hole through the greenhouse which bordered the animal pen. Once inside, Wagner feasted on several thousand dollars' worth of delicate, and obviously tasty, young plants. Doyle was livid, and for one of the few times I'd seen, speechless. He slowly spun around taking in the carnage when—WHAM! Wager rammed headlong into Doyle's back.

"You mother!" In one fell swoop, Doyle grabbed a shovel leaned near the greenhouse's front door. The boss swung downward just as Wagner lunged a second time. The metal rung out, and Wagner hit the ground. For the briefest of seconds, I thought maybe the goat was simply knocked out, but then I heard it, the gurgling death rattle. Wagner kicked his legs a few times, coughed up a handful of foamy blood, and lay still.

Doyle took one look at the dead goat and then called the Mexican guys who lived behind the store. A deal was struck. The men dug a hole back near the greenhouse. They started a fire in the pit. They prepared Wagner's body then rubbed his meat with spices and encased him in wet burlap.

Our Spanish-speaking customers called it Cabrito, smoked goat meat.

Wagner cooked on the smoldering embers buried in the ground all that day and part of the next. I will confess to enjoying the meal we made of his flesh. Many of our customers did, as well. Some even knew Wagner before his untimely death, though Doyle kept the identity of our meaty meal secret, lest the day ever came when Ginger returned to claim her pet.

One day, after having been gone several months, she finally did that very thing.

I was not present at the time, but Doyle told me she sobbed as he explained a pack of dogs had gotten into the enclosure and killed poor Wagner. She found some comfort once he led her outside, and showed her the hole he claimed to be Wagner's final resting place. Had Ginger looked closely, she would have spotted the bits of charred wood scattered about. She would have realized the hole was not a grave, but an earthen oven. Not Wagner's final resting space, but the place where his flesh and bones were slow-roasted until a golden, juicy brown.

Gruesome as eating Wagner may sound, the partaking of his body was not the most morbid of my experiences at Pearl's. That distinction came via Doyle's kinfolk. Family tree? Nope. Doyle's lineage sprang from a stump. A gnarly piece of wood with its roots firmly embedded in the blood-red dirt of Oklahoma. One by one, members of his clan made their way to Pearl's for the family discount. Cousins, aunts, uncles, and in-laws. They didn't venture to Texas often, but when they did they always left a memorable impression.

One cousin even worked with us for awhile. She was a plain looking woman in her mid-thirties. Married with three kids that even in the dead of summer had yellow, snot-crusted nostrils and ratty heads of hair. Except when someone had given them a fresh buzz cut. Eloise was her name and she lived in fear of producing a fourth mouth to feed. She'd had her tubes tied after the last baby, but every other month she was convinced her husband's sperm had kidnapped a few of her eggs and fertilized them not in her womb, but in her fallopian tube.

Eloise would cry and caterwaul, "I have a tubal pregnancy. I just know I do," for several days. Eventually the event she was so desperately waiting for would arrive. At which point, Eloise would smile and say, "Auntie Em finally showed up to paint my room."

Then there were the Siamese twins. Okay, they weren't actually twins, having been born ten months apart, but despite the three-hundred days separating their entrance into the world, I am and forever will be convinced the brothers shared but a single brain. No connective tissue bound them together, so I'm not sure how the gelatinous organ worked, but whenever one brother spoke the other could manage nothing more than a Beavis and Butthead-style laugh. Many a time their shared brain ceased to work at all and the pair emitted a simultaneous duet of hollow, huh, a huh, huh, huhs.

The brothers ended up marrying two sisters. Women who must have outweighed them by two hundred pounds each. Women who possessed thick, albeit downy—at least it looked soft—black mustaches. Women whose stunning ugliness was overshadowed only by their nasty temperaments. I went with Doyle to the Justice of the Peace to witness the nuptials. The brothers giggled, huh-a-huh-huh-huh, all the way through the vows. I can't help but wonder if they are still laughing all these years later.

However, it was a distant relative, a great uncle, I do believe, who provided the most unique experience. The uncle worked for a funeral home somewhere in the Sooner state. Where in particular I better not say, but this uncle showed up one day in a long black hearse. He'd been dispatched over to Albuquerque to fetch some Okie who had gone over to New Mexico for a mountain vacation. The Okie had consumed a few too many adult beverages and discovered the hard way that taking mountain curves at a hundred and ten is detrimental to your health. Passing through Amarillo with the deceased, the uncle decided he might as well stock up on dog food and sweet grain for his goats at the family discount price.

Loading the feed, it unnerved me to stack the five sacks of dry dog food alongside the sleek silver casket. But I was downright perplexed when I ran out of room and still had the four bags of sweet grain. Doyle's uncle came outside smoking a cigarette as I stared at the load. I finally decided to stack the goat feed on the passenger seat, but the uncle stopped me.

Flicking the smoking cigarette butt into the street he said, "Just stack that shit up on top. I don't wanna ride all the way back to Oklahoma with it up front."

I'd seen a spray of roses, but never one of paper feedsacks.

Speaking of roses, Doyle continued to lust after the legal secretary bearing that name. Without a legal quandary giving him good reason to maintain contact, he worked hard to keep close. First, he had a will drawn up, even though he had little to leave behind. Then he inquired about suing his neighbors when their dog impregnated Snuggles.

Despite all the arranged liaisons and the high-priced artificial inseminations, the bulldog had failed to conceive, so after investing several thousand dollars and better than three years to the endeavor, Doyle finally gave up on the bitch ever having pups. At her very next cycle, his neighbor's mutt jumped the fence and knocked her up. Doyle was pissed, but he knew full-well the owners had nothing to sue for. Nevertheless, the notion gave him reason to visit the lawyer's office and spend more time with Rose.

Despite his infatuation and all his efforts, Rose refused to go out on a date with my boss. Doyle claimed to be wearing her down, but I could tell her constant and unyielding rejections were leaving him unnerved and uncharacteristically insecure.

Asking her out for what had to be the fiftieth time, and hearing yet another "no," he patted his stomach and said, "Maybe I'm getting fat?" From that point on, he took to doing crunches back in the sack room.

Unable to believe her reluctance stemmed from anything other than his appearance, Doyle went through several looks that summer. Tom Selleck-esque mustache, no mustache, fu Manchu mustache. Goatee, long hair, short hair. Nothing garnered Rose's favor. And truth be told, I think he lost sight of her as a person over those months. She became a goal, a mountain peak to scale, and the fact he couldn't gain a single foothold unraveled him.

I knew how Doyle felt. It was that summer after my high school graduation that I too began to fray. Once upon a time going to work had been the highlight of my day. The very thing I looked forward to the most, but I'd heard all of Doyle's jokes. I knew which of his stories were complete bullshit, and which ones were tied to a thread of truth.

In short, I'd stopped having fun. To be fair, that was the case away from Pearl's as well. My buddies all had kids, and jobs, and plans for the future. I wanted to have a plan. I wanted to head out to far West Texas and attend Sul Ross State University. I wanted to study wildlife biology, but lack of money and family obligations rendered that impossible. I had my pig money. I could have struck off for Alpine over on the far western side of Texas. My winnings would have funded a couple of semesters' worth of school at Sul Ross, but to do so would have left my mom high and dry. And what if I didn't find a job out there? What if I ran out of money and had to come crawling back after my freshman year? I'd told Doyle what I wanted to do, and he'd made it clear he thought my dreams were nonsense.

"College ain't all it's cracked up to be," he said. "Damn

teachers are usually a bunch of fucking liberals. They don't know the first thing about the real world."

Doyle had been on a tirade against liberals ever since Ann Richards, a Democrat and a female Democrat to boot, had taken office as Texas governor the previous January.

"Hell," he said. "You might be smart and all, but you don't belong in a college dorm any more than I do. Sign up for a good technical school and you can be making some real money this time next year."

All of it kept me right where I was. The anxiety of striking out on my own. The need to help support my family. The fear that Doyle was right. Looking back now I can see that summer was the beginning of the end. My days at Pearl's Feed and Seed were limited. Especially the good ones, as from that point on I resented my fate. I resented the fact that I lacked the courage to chase my dreams. I resented Doyle for continuing to have fun. Maybe it was my attitude that turned Doyle. Maybe it was his sexual frustration over Rose. Maybe we'd spent too many months together in each other's company, there in that dusty fly-specked store. But it was that summer when our relationship began its descent. Though hard to define, the connection had always been more than employer/employee. Mere friends? Mentor/greenhorn? Teacher/pupil? Older/younger brother?

I suppose all of them fit at one time or another, but it only takes two words to describe what we soon became.

Feudal combatants.

Chapter Seventeen

Ring My Bell

The first time Doyle fired me, it was a stormy rain-sodden afternoon. Days like that are rare in the dry Texas Panhandle. Doubly so in late August, when the majority of lawns have long since turned yellow under the summer's relentless heat. But the sun wasn't out that particular day. Low-hanging gray clouds dominated the sky. Thunder rumbled, and the occasional flash of lighting lit up the store.

Only a handful of customers had wandered in the entire day, and not a single once since lunch. Doyle and I had gambled until we were sick of passing each other's money back and forth. By early afternoon we had nothing to do other than stare out Pearl's dirty front window. A few cars passed by, their tires hissing against the wet asphalt.

Finally Doyle broke the silence and said, "What I need is some pussy."

In an effort to project a more stable and wholesome self-image, he'd curtailed his sexual activity in the past few months. Not stopped, but certainly slowed. Rose had finally confessed to Doyle she'd heard far too many stories about him from her boss. With both a young daughter and an impressionable son from a previous marriage, she refused to date anyone who couldn't be a good role model. Those moral obligations might have been enough to scare my boss off, if Rose hadn't made the mistake of adding one more line. "Regardless of how attractive I find you to be, I can't risk entering a relationship with someone I can't invite home to meet my kids."

Doyle analyzed the shit out of that statement. He took what he wanted from her words, rearranged them, and tossed out the rest. She found him attractive and would invite him over for a night of fun, once he proved he was respectable. He stopped going to The Caravan and all other bars. He started going to church on days besides Easter and Christmas. And he turned down offers from several women for a bit of fun.

I should make one thing clear. He didn't turn over a new leaf. His mindset and his goals did not change. Only his outward behavior. He invited Rose to church not so much because he wanted her to sit beside him in a pew, but because he wanted her to know he was going. He told his lawyer that he'd quit drinking and gambling, in hopes the man would pass the lies on to Rose. And he sent her flowers every week. Sent as in paid a florist to deliver them. I badgered him about his time-honored method of stealing them while the girl looked on. Doyle simply told me to shut the hell up and mind my own business. Each week he spent countless hours trying to create a romantic note to go along with the blooms.

Looking back now, it's not lost on me that our roles had reversed. At least regarding my unrequited obsession with Samantha Blake and his fool-hearted pursuit of the ever-reluctant Rose. Suddenly, he was trying desperately to find an angle, an opening, and I was the one tossing out careless advice.

"Quit sending her roses," I said one day. "Her name is Rose. I bet every guy who's ever tried to get in her pants has sent roses. Pick a batch of dandelions and send to her. Then write, *You are the only Rose for me. Every other rose is but a weed next to your beauty.*

I was trying to be funny, sarcastic even, but Doyle, looked up and said, "Hey, that's pretty good. And next week I can send daisies or something else a lot cheaper than roses without looking like a tightwad."

Of course you can't order a batch of dandelions through FTD, so Doyle made me hand deliver them. Hell of it was. She bought it. Rose finally agreed to go out on a date.

"A single date. Nothing more," she added.

Of course that one "yes" turned Doyle's thoughts to the next quest.

"The rain always makes me horny," he said, as the water dripped through our leaky ceiling and into a well-placed five-gallon bucket. I knew he was thinking about Rose. About their scheduled date that night. Rose refused to let him pick her up at her house, so they were instead going to meet at a restaurant. But she had a deposition and wasn't sure what time she would get free. As the afternoon ticked along, Doyle moved his stool closer and closer to the phone.

Around three he picked it up and immediately started cussing. "Fucking thing isn't working. No dial tone." He jiggled the button on the receiver. Nothing. He checked the cord heading into wall. Unplugged it several times and then listened again. "Motherfucker!"

I suppressed a grin. Months of work and planning, only to get cock-blocked by Ma Bell.

"What the hell are grinning about?"

I shrugged. "The rain makes you horny, it makes me smile."

"Bullshit. You think it's fucking funny the phone is out and now I'm not gonna get laid."

"You weren't going to get laid anyway. She said a date. Nothing more. Remember?"

Doyle went through all the same gyrations trying to make the phone work.

"You think a woman who's spent months saying no is gonna suddenly start saying yes to everything?"

"Shut-up and go next door. See if their phone is working."

"In the rain?"

"Damn right, in the rain. You ain't gonna fucking melt."

Next door was actually a full block away. An auto mechanic's shop that sat a good hundred yards to our east. And the guy who owned the joint wasn't the friendliest fella around.

"You're serious?"

"Hell yeah, I'm serious," the boss answered. "And if their phone is working call the law office and tell them to give Rose a message my phone is out."

I trudged over and discovered that yeah, their phone was working. Carrying out my mission, I headed back to Pearl's knowing the boss wasn't going to like what I had to say. Still pissed I'd gotten drenched just because Doyle was trying to get his pecker wet, I looked forward to jacking with his emotions.

"Well?" he asked when I walked in and sat down without speaking a word.

I shrugged. "Well, what?"

"You know damned good and well what. Is their phone working?"

"Yep."

"Did you call?"

"Yep."

The veins in Doyle's neck bulged. "What the fuck did they say?"

I listened to several drips land in the bucket before I answered, "They said Rose was at a deposition."

"I already knew that damn much."

"The receptionist took the message, but she doubts Rose comes back to the office before Monday morning."

"You're shitting me?"

"Would I shit you? You're my favorite turd." The saying was one of Doyle's favorites, but it didn't make him smile.

"Fuck!" Doyle banged his fist on the counter.

Pacing around the room, he twice picked up the phone to listen for a dial tone. Finally he stepped outside. I watched him head for the alley. He was gone only a few minutes before he stepped way out near the street and stared up at our roof. His feet were now muddy and he left soggy brown piles on the pavement everywhere he stepped. He didn't bother to wipe his boots when he came back inside. I stared at the mess, knowing I would be the one to clean it up, but turns out, the boss had an even worse plans for me.

Doyle went to the back and began rummaging through the old sewing stuff his mom had left behind. After a bit he came back up front with an odd rigged-up contraption. He'd taken three thick cardboard tubes that bolts of fabric had been wound around, and using duct tape and some strips of elastic material to bind the tubes, he'd created a makeshift tripod.

"The phone line is sagging down and touching the roof," he explained. "Bet it's shorting out against the wet metal."

I said nothing.

"Go get the ladder," the boss said. "And then climb up there and prop it up with this."

I folded my arms across my chest. "Not in the rain."

Doyle shook his head. "Don't start that shit again. You

ain't gonna melt. Now get the ladder and haul your ass up there."

A low, rolling growl of thunder filled the silence.

I didn't move.

"What the fuck you waiting for?"

"You to come to your senses."

We stared at each other until I felt obligated to defend my mutinous attitude. "The rain is bad enough, but do you really expect me take an aluminum ladder out into a thunderstorm, and use it to climb up on top of a slick, metal roof. While it's lightening?"

"Don't be a puss. It's barely drizzling and it's all cloud-to-cloud lightening."

"I don't give a shit what it is. I'm not doing it," I said. "What kind of moron climbs on a wet roof and grabs a power line?"

"It's a phone line." Doyle's contemptuous tone made it clear only an idiot would be afraid of a measly phone line. "It only has juice when someone is actually calling."

"Well, I hope nobody calls while you're up there jacking with it, 'cause I'm staying right here, where it's dry and I don't have to worry about getting my ass fried."

"Would you rather get your ass fired?"

"Guess so."

Doyle nodded, walked over to the cash register, and counted out a hundred and twenty bucks. He shoved the bills against my chest. "There you go. That covers what I owe you. Either get up on the roof, or take your money and get out."

I eyed him. "You serious?"

"As a fucking heart attack."

Pocketing the money, I walked out the door just as the rain picked up. My truck's windshield wipers kept time with my pounding heart as I drove away. I couldn't believe Doyle had fired me just like that. And for something so stupid. Only an idiot would climb up on that roof. It was fucking raining. The ladder and the roof were metal. There was lighting. I didn't for a second regret my decision, but what the hell was I going to do for a job? My college classes started in two weeks. Hopefully I could find one that would let me work around my schedule. I'd had everything worked out with Doyle, but that was before he tossed me aside for a girl. For a damned phone call from a girl.

I drove around that night looking for any of my friends to hang with, but found only a couple of guys I knew, and none I could truly call a friend. I circled by the old Bailloux place, even though John had moved out west of town to live with a cousin, and Candy was still off in sunny Florida. The weeds around their house had grown taller and the cars rustier. Or so it seemed in my dour mood. I even pulled up outside the gate of the ag farm. I tried to go inside but somebody had changed the lock and seeing as to how I was no longer an FFA student, I had no clue as to the new combination. Nearly a year to the day had passed since I'd brought Darcy to the farm.

Finally, sometime around midnight, I headed for Brent's house. By that time his daughter was already a year old, and he'd been married nearly that long. He'd stuck it out and graduated, but I rarely saw him since he held two jobs to support his family. His car wasn't in the driveway, but the lights were on so I stopped anyway.

I knocked gently so as not to wake his kid. His wife, Lisa, answered. Seeing me, she tucked a strand of dirty blond hair behind her ear. "Brent's not here," she whispered.

"Yeah, that's what I figured since his car was gone. But I saw the light and thought I'd stop anyway."

I'd been over to their place enough to know Lisa's housekeeping skills were shaky at best. She and Brent had three or four big dogs, which she insisted on letting run around the place. Tonight the aroma of dog shit was pungent enough for me to detect there on the porch.

"Brent's working the graveyard shift out at Blue Beacon," Lisa said. "He won't be home until morning, but you can come in and stay awhile if you want. The baby is asleep. We can have a few beers ... *together.*"

Lisa had a nice body, but not the prettiest face in the world. Even uglier still was her reputation for cheating on Brent. I was mad, lonely, and probably a bit depressed that night. I'd knocked on the door in desperate need of a friend. I could tell by the way Lisa said *together* that she was in as bad a need of company as me. I took a deep breath, letting the dog shit tainted air fill first my nostrils, then my lungs. I held the breath while I pondered the possibilities.

"That's okay," I finally answered. "I should be getting home anyway."

That night, on the way home, I believed only the smell had kept me from going inside. I thought my willpower had originated in my nose, but all these years later I know it took more than that for me to walk away.

Doyle would have gone in.

Olfactory senses be damned. He'd have worn a clothespin if he'd had to, but he would have taken Lisa's offer. He would have slept with his friend's wife as easily as he had tossed our friendship to fire me over a girl. Over a measly damned phone call from a girl!

And I might have as well on another night. But on that night, I wanted to be anything but like Doyle Suggs.

Chapter Eighteen

So Long Fatboy

I heard the phone ringing, but no way in hell was I climbing out of bed to answer. Not when it'd been several years since I'd last had the opportunity to sleep in on a Saturday morning. My bedroom door opened before I had a chance to drift back into dreamland. The cordless handset landed on my chest with a dull thud.

"Next time, get up to answer your own calls." My brother didn't bother to shut the door on his way out.

"Hello?" I croaked

"Where are you?" Doyle asked.

"In bed."

"Well, get the hell up," he said. "You're already an hour late."

"You fired me. Remember?"

"Ahh … bullshit. Haven't you worked for me long enough to know when I'm jerking your chain?"

Rubbing the sleep from my eyes, I squinted toward the window. Bright sunlight streamed through the cracks in the blinds, so no doubt the rain clouds had moved on. "I'm still not climbing up on that roof."

"Nobody asked you to. Phone's working today. How soon 'til you get here?"

"Forty-five minutes. Maybe an hour," I said.

"An hour? What are you, a teenage girl? Get your ass out of bed, grab your keys, and I'll see you in fifteen."

"I gotta take a shower."

"Don't bother," Doyle said. "The chicken truck is here."

Hanging up, I laid there for several minutes, pondering. Did I really want to get up and head back to the feed store, for what would amount to a horrible day, doing the very worst duty at the joint?

The chicken truck came from a hatchery over in New Mexico. A semi pulling a full-sized flatbed trailer stacked full of plastic crates, the chicken truck came once a year. Inside each and every one of those crates were eight to ten laying hens. The truck carried something in the neighborhood of two hundred crates. Doyle would buy at least half the load as he did every August, when the hatchery sold off their excess stock. Unloading and emptying all those cluckers was a dirty, nasty job. To promote airflow, the crates were slotted, top, sides and bottom. The chickens fortunate enough to be stacked on top were lucky. Without birds above them, they remained relatively clean. However, the second row of hens, and every row below, was subjected to the falling shit of their upstairs brethren.

Chicken crap is rank, runny, and rampantly produced. As the saying goes, shit runs downhill, so the fowl at the bottom of the load were indeed quite foul. After their two-hour journey from the hatchery they would literally be dripping with filth. Pulling such a wet, smelly hen from its plastic crate was not a chore I looked forward to.

But I'll give Doyle credit. He hadn't disguised the task ahead of me. He hadn't promised rose petals and hand jobs if I returned to work. He hadn't lied, tricked, or cajoled me into coming back. More than anything else, that convinced me to toss back the covers and head in to reclaim my position at Pearl's Feed and Seed. An hour later, I regretted my decision.

Pecked. Pooped upon. Perpetually pestered.

Why the hell had I returned, knowing it was going to be that way? With each moist and slimy chicken, I questioned my sanity.

Doyle was up front, taking care of the usual customers, but I wasn't without an audience as the arrival of the chicken truck was a big event for a particular slice of our clientèle.

Drive an ice cream truck through the middle of a fat camp, and you might get a semblance of the urgency and excitement that the chicken truck instilled among the Vietnamese, Laotian, and Cambodian customers that thought of Pearl's as more of a meat market than a feed store. They came in hordes, not the least bit deterred by the sight or stench of feces dripping from their prospective dinner. They pushed, yelled, and fought for what they deemed the choicest, plump and juicy hens.

Unstacking five crates at a time from the semi, I'd load the containers on a two-wheeled dolly and haul them back to the animal enclosure. The crowd of shoppers, mostly middle-aged to older women, would surround me, making it hard to maneuver the dolly. Being August, it was already hot enough without a crew of people pressing in close to inspect the chickens. The humidity from the previous day's rain made the air almost suffocating. The birds themselves were scared and nervous from their truck ride. No doubt the throng of chattering and excited women reaching, poking, and prodding added to the hens' fear. Huddled in the corners, the animals used their feet to cling to the crate, making it tough to extract them. If the hen appeared the least bit savory, one of the women would snatch the bird right from my grimy hands.

The truck took several hours to unload, but the chicken euphoria lasted only for thirty or forty-five minutes. After that it was just me and the birds and a smattering of customers wandering out back to check out the new stock.

Why all those Asian women felt compelled to fight over a few particular birds when we'd have five- or six hundred was beyond me. Doyle charged an extra dollar per bird for as long as the frenzy lasted, so he loved to see them. I, however, was glad when all the women departed, taking their stuffed gunny sacks with them.

Lunch time had arrived by the time I finished unloading our half of the truck. The animal enclosure was a sea of clucking chickens. My jeans were wet from the knees down, my shirt flecked with bits of chicken shit, and my hair matted with sweat and God-knows-what else. But finally, I headed inside for a cold Dr Pepper and a chance to wash my hands and face.

"Ordered us a pizza," Doyle said when I took a seat at the counter. Buying my lunch was his version of a peace offering. An apology of sorts, at least in his mind. I wondered if Rose had ever gotten a hold of him. If they had gone on their date. I wasn't about to bring the whole phone thing up, but luckily Doyle didn't keep me in suspense.

"You were right," Doyle said after a few minutes. "I didn't get laid. Not even close."

Sipping my Dr Pepper, I said nothing.

"A fucking peck on the cheek. That's all I got. Between our meals and her three glasses of wine, it only cost me seventy bucks."

I tried not to grin.

"Hell, I couldn't even order myself a beer since I told her I quit drinking. But I ain't giving up. Hell no. I'm gonna get some of that, come hell or high water."

After spending the entire morning unloading all those hens, I spent the afternoon, the really hot part of the day, trying to recatch the very same chickens for various customers. Some customers only wanted one, others bought a dozen or so. Some planned to eat their purchase, while others hoped to have a steady supply of fresh eggs. Most of the time, Doyle sold the prospective buyers a gunny sack to carry away their animals, but a few brought cages or crates from home.

The sun was high in the sky when Hong showed up. Hong was a regular customer. A chicken fighter, a bookie, a man who seemed to have his finger in a lot of pies. No doubt several of them illegal. Including some kind of backyard kickboxing operation. He talked about his fights often, and in my mind I imagined scenes reminiscent of the old Clint Eastwood movie, *Every Which Way But Loose*, only with Asian martial arts fighters, rather than tough middle-class workers.

I'm not sure of Hong's country of origin, but he spoke in broken English, unless he really needed to get his point across. At which point he talked without an accent and in terms anyone could understand.

Hong was a short man of barely more than five feet. He had a large, rounded belly, flabby pock-marked cheeks, and a mostly bald head, which he attempted to cover with thin wisps of hair combed over from just above his right ear. He wore gaudy gold chains around his fleshy neck and a huge pinky ring adorned with diamonds in the shape of a lucky horseshoe. The man spent a lot of money at Pearl's, but even Doyle found him pompous and obnoxious. More often than not, Hong brought a posse with him, but on this day he was without the three or four unpleasant looking Asian youths who usually accompanied him. I always presumed them to be in his stable of kickboxers.

"Big fight tonight," he said. "Partner from Dallas bringing his fighters. Hear you have chickens. Need twenty-five, maybe thirty to feed crowd."

Doyle said, "Travis, go catch Hong thirty birds."

To aid in the capture of the chickens we used a long, four-foot piece of rigid wire bent into a V at the end. Reaching out you could snare the skinny part of a hen's leg in that V, and by maintaining tension drag them back to you. The maneuver is easier said than done, but it still beat catching the squawking birds by hand.

I'd nabbed five hens and stowed them safely in a gunny sack before Hong ventured outside to join me. Sweat ran into my eyes as I scooped up a sixth. The outdoor thermometer nailed to the greenhouse frame read a hundred and five.

"That one no good." Hong pointed to the flapping red hen I was about to stuff in a second sack. "Too skinny."

I reluctantly let it go and went after another. In the meantime, Hong untied the string and opened the burlap bag I'd already filled.

"Too skinny." He let go one hen. "Too skinny, too skinny, too old." He dumped the entire contents. "And no black birds. They too stringy."

"Hey," I said. "You know how hard it was to catch those?"

"Why I care," Hong said. "I paying customer. You do as I say." He poked himself in the chest.

Twenty minutes later we had a grand total of four birds bagged. The other dozen I'd caught had been deemed unacceptable. Sweat stung my eyes and soaked my shirt. I knew

Hong had to be hot as well, as perspiration had beaded on his balding head. And yet, he kept rejecting my selections.

"You no sweat like that if in better shape," he said.

"Screw you," I answered. "I'm in better shape than you."

"Hey, Fatboy. I paying customer. No disrespect me." He shook his head at my latest capture.

I glared at him.

"Want me tell boss you being asshole, Fatboy?"

"I don't give a shit what you do." I lunged and grabbed a black hen. Without looking at Hong, I stuffed the bird into a sack.

"You deaf, Fatboy? I already say no black birds. They too stringy."

"Guess what, I'm done screwing around out here. It's too damned hot to keep chasing these chickens around just so you can toss them back."

"Who the paying customer here? Me, that's who. You catch as many birds as I say. Fatboy." He spat the last word and followed it with a devilish grin. Now I'll admit. The beers my buddies and I consumed every weekend had started to thicken my middle by that point, but compared to Hong, I was a regular Adonis. And I was damn sick of him calling me Fatboy.

"Tell you what, *Fatman*." I stared Hong right in the eye. "I'm gonna keep catching these chickens until we have thirty, but the first one you let go, I'm done. After that you can catch your own damn birds."

He didn't blink or look away, but he didn't argue either. Fifteen minutes later, I had twenty hens stuffed in four burlap bags.

Ten more to go.

Hong hadn't said a word, but he kept looking at his watch.

Despite the heat and the physical effort it took to catch the chickens, my heart rate subsided, as did my anger and agitation. But then, when I filled the fifth sack with what was the twenty-fifth bird, Hong stepped over and said, "Those no good." In one motion he dumped the last five hens I'd caught.

He made a sweeping motion with his right hand. "Catch again, Fatboy."

"I'm done." Tossing the rigid wire pole at his feet, I said, "Catch the rest yourself."

"You no walk away from me, Fatboy." Hong grabbed the back of my shirt and gave it a hard yank.

I spun and grabbed two handfuls of his shirt. Shoving him against the wall, I said, "You have a problem with catching your own damn birds? Even after I told you not to let any more go?" I gave him a little shake. "Huh? Do you?"

Hong stared up at me with wide, frightened eyes. He was more than a foot shorter than me and nowhere near as strong. I felt his flabby man-boobs pressing against the back side of my knuckles.

"No. No problem whatsoever. I was just playing around.

Having a bit of fun at your expense. My apologies," he said without a single trace of his usual broken speech pattern.

I stomped inside, grabbed another cold Dr Pepper, and sat down directly beneath the cool flow of air conditioning.

"Where's Hong?" Doyle asked.

"Outside. Catching his own fucking chickens," I said.

Doyle arched a brow. I could tell he wanted to smile, even though he suppressed the actual grin. Another fifteen minutes leaked by before Hong came inside, carrying a burlap bag in each hand. Looking at me he said, "You mind helping me carry out the other sacks?"

"Nope. Not at all."

After I'd loaded them into Hong's van, I ventured back inside. Hong grinned at me.

"You big strong boy," he said back to his usual vernacular. "Come fight for me tonight. I pay you five hundred. Fans like big bad white boy to hate."

"Not me. Maybe Doyle will do it. He could use the money for his next date."

The boss raised his hands in the air. "I'm a lover, not a fighter."

"That's not what Rose said," I countered.

"Fuck you," Doyle shot back.

"Oh, ha ha ha. You funny guys," Hong said. "Who this Rose?"

"My girlfriend," Doyle answered.

"Only she doesn't know it," I said.

Rather than respond to me, the boss turned to Hong. "You only missed it by five minutes. I'll wager you double or nothing that next time you can keep him out there in the heat chasing chickens like a dumb ass for the whole hour."

Hong shook his head. "No next time for me. Your bet's too dangerous." He laughed. "Fatboy might hit me I try that again."

The two men brayed like the jackasses they were.

And that's when I quit ... the first time. But sometimes good things are born from bad situations.

Doyle fired me on Friday for refusing to climb on that roof. I quit on Saturday for being used as a pawn in a stupid bet. Later that night, or to be more exact, an hour into Sunday morning, I found myself handcuffed, sitting in the back of a patrol car. Sitting there in that cruiser, I believed my luck had gone from bad to worse. Little did I know, my scrape with the law was going to be the luckiest event of my life.

Chapter Nineteen

Fuzzy Wuzzy Wuz A Dumbass

How I came to be handcuffed and stuffed into the back of that deputy's car is quite the sad tale.

I drove away from Doyle, and Hong, and my job at Pearl's Feed and Seed, desperate not to spend another lonesome night, lest I wind up a second time on Lisa's front porch. I didn't trust my willpower to do the right thing two nights in a row.

That desperation forced me to call up Candy Bailloux's favorite fellatio fellow, Steve Golds. I hadn't hung out with Steve in a long time, because he now lived in an apartment with a guy I couldn't stand.

Freddie Brown had gone to school at Caprock as well. Like Steve, he was a year ahead of me. Freddie had hung out at the Baillouxs' some, but he and I never had gotten along. He was the kind of guy who had to be the center of attention and didn't care if he had to lie, steal, or beg to garner the spotlight. Since school he'd gained another hundred pounds, grown a scraggly beard on his third chin, and become all the more obnoxious.

Steve's daughter was right at a year old, but he only had her every other weekend. When I called, he said this wasn't the weekend, so I headed over to his and Freddie's place, despite my misgivings about the latter.

Shortly after I arrived, another guy we'd gone to school with, a short, skinny fella named Chad Jones, showed up. Chad had perhaps the world's largest Adam's apple, but girls loved him. He was also funny as hell, so his being there sort of offset Freddie's presence.

We decided as a group to buy some beer and head to this teen dance club out south of town. A place called Footloose. The joint was just as cheesy and unoriginal as its name, but Chad had promised two different girls that he would show up. The rest of us knew Chad would know a dozen other girls to introduce us to. Besides, we weren't old enough to get in any of the real bars in town. At least not any that attracted members of the opposite sex.

We did however know of a seedy little liquor store over in a bad section of Amarillo that would sell us beer. I was the youngest in the group, but also the tallest. That fact alone led the guys to nominate me to go inside and buy the booze.

"Freddie is nearly as tall," I pointed out. "And he's a year older than me. Besides he has a beard."

Chad grabbed the ten or twelve curly hairs sprouting from Freddie's third chin. "You call this a beard? I got more hair growing wild around my asshole than he does on this dewlap."

Freddie slapped his hand away. "Fuck you. Least I'm tall enough to ride the roller coaster at the fair."

"I vote for you, Travis," Steve said. "If you hadn't quit your damned job we coulda got your boss to buy us beer, so it's your fault we had to drive all the way over to the hood."

Just like that I was elected to go in and buy a twelve pack. The guys wanted Coors Light, but I was doing the buying so I chose Budweiser as their punishment for making me venture inside. Freddie threw a fit when I exited the store and proudly hoisted the box for all to see.

"I'm not drinking that shit," he said. "What are we, Mexicans?"

"Beer is beer," Steve said.

In a huff, Freddie stormed inside and bought not the Coors Light he'd supposedly wanted, but a four-pack of fuzzy navel flavored wine coolers. He claimed they were for any chicks we picked up, but Freddie ended up drinking three of the bottles on the way to the club. Tossing the empties at passing road signs, he wasn't anywhere near coordinated enough to hit any of them. Steve did peg a yield sign with a balled-up Bud can, but then again I'd slowed down as we passed through that particular intersection.

Me? I didn't have a single sip of beer before we arrived. I didn't want to take the chance of getting caught drinking and driving. In the parking lot the guys finished off their beverages while I downed a quick one to catch up. Hiding the empties along with half a dozen full cans under the back seat of my truck, we climbed out.

Freddie, his bladder full of Bartles and Jaymes fuzzy navels, stepped behind my pickup to relieve the pressure. I had no idea he set his last wine cooler in the bed of my Ford until the cops showed.

Travis Erwin! Travis Erwin! Please come to the front. Travis Erwin!

I couldn't imagine why I was being paged, but I excused myself from the girl I'd been two-stepping with and headed to see what was up.

A Randall County sheriff's deputy greeted me at the door.

When I identified myself as Travis Erwin, he led me outside where a second officer held up a bottle. An inch of orange liquid sat in the bottom of the glass container.

"Does this belong to you?"

I shook my head. "No, sir."

"Can you explain how it came to be in the bed of your truck?"

I paused. I hadn't lied when I said the wine cooler wasn't mine, but now I was forced to either lie or rat out Freddie.

"I assume," the officer pointed at my pickup, "that is your truck since it's registered in your name."

Doyle's voice whispered in my ear. *Never assume anything, it only makes an ass out of you and me.* I was smart enough to realize now was not the time to go quoting my boss's, I mean former boss's, favorite sayings.

"Yes, sir. It's mine. And I guess someone put that bottle in there."

"Someone, huh." The first cop shined a flashlight directly in my eyes. "You been drinking, son?"

Several hours had gone by since I'd consumed that one beer. And I'd been inside dancing and sweating. I'd even taken a leak since. Surely that one Budweiser had long left the building. Confident I could lie and get away with it, I said, "No, sir, I haven't been drinking."

The officers put me through a dozen tests over the next twenty minutes. Walking a line. Touching my nose. Standing on one foot. After every challenge they asked me again if I'd been drinking. I provided the same answer every time.

In the meantime, I watched as a group of seven or eight officers roamed the parking lot, looking in the backs of trucks and shining their lights into the interiors. Apparently a lot of vehicles contained booze, as they paged half a dozen other unlucky participants to come outside. I was grateful we'd hidden our stash under the seat.

I managed to perform every task the deputy requested and just when I thought freedom was at hand, he said, "Okay, hand me your keys."

"My keys?"

He nodded. "If I don't find anymore bottles hidden in your vehicle, you can go back inside and have fun."

The cop was lying. Despite the fact he wouldn't find any bottles in my truck, I knew he wouldn't let me go back in the club. He wouldn't find any bottles, but when he discovered all those beer cans, my fun for the night was gonna be long gone.

He did.

It was.

And that's how I wound up handcuffed in the back of a patrol car. But don't shed any tears for me, for without those hefty fines and the need to speak to a lawyer I wouldn't have ventured back to the feed store.

I wouldn't have begged Doyle for my job back.

I wouldn't have met Vail Peterson.

I wouldn't have fallen in love.

Chapter Twenty

Cupid's Safety Pin

Before I fell in love, I fell in lust. Clarissa Cates was her name. I noticed her the day my college classes began. That was a Tuesday. I didn't have trigonometry class again for another two days. When Thursday rolled around I made a point to sit beside her. We made eye contact as I took my seat, but the professor began his lecture before I thought of anything to say. For the next hour and fifteen minutes I listened to the man drone on about the Pythagorean Theorem while Clarissa and I exchanged smiles.

"I like your cowboy boots," she said when class was over.

"I like your blue eyes," I answered back.

We went to lunch that afternoon. Dinner on Friday, and Sunday morning I left her apartment as the sun broke the eastern horizon.

Clarissa was two years older than me. She was from Lubbock, two hours south of Amarillo. She'd attended Texas Tech University in her hometown, but too much partying had placed her first, on academic probation, then on suspension. Her father, a district judge, set her up with an apartment and a generous stipend so Clarissa could devote her full attention to repairing her dismal grade point average without the distraction of a job getting in the way.

I suppose he considered Amarillo College too small of a school and the city itself too dull to enable Clarissa's more festive side. For a judge, he wasn't all that bright. And while it is doubtful a high-brow man of his stature will ever read this tomè, I do believe I'll avoid Lubbock just in case. I met the judge only once. He made it painfully obvious he didn't like the idea of me distracting his daughter. Nor was he impressed by the fact I'd been raised by a single mother who worked as a hairdresser. Or that I labored at a feed store. Or was majoring in Natural Science at Amarillo College.

The man's bushy white eyebrows climbed higher on his liver spotted forehead each time I answered one of his questions. He would've shit a brick had I told him even a fraction of what went on at Pearl's, or of my recent adventure with the judicial system.

Even without those tales, Clarissa's dad spoke his mind. I survived a meal at her parents' house, but as Clarissa and I were leaving, her dad tossed her a quarter and said, "Keep that handy."

"Why, Daddy?"

The man did not look at his daughter. Instead he stared straight at me and said, "So when you are out on a date with that boy, and finally come to your senses, you can call someone to come pick you up."

Clarissa and I had a lot of fun together, though our relationship was doomed. But let me back up, to the aftermath of the errant fuzzy navel bottle.

To his credit, Doyle gave me my job back without too much teasing. Second, third, fourth chances. He'd needed quite a few do-overs in his own life, and while Doyle was a lot of things, a hypocrite was not one of them.

The boss found the tale of my legal woes quite interesting. I hadn't actually gotten arrested, but only because I passed all of the sobriety tests, and blew well below the legal limit on the breathalyzer.

Despite those facts, and for reasons not thoroughly explained to me, the officer still ticketed me for public intoxication. Tacked on to that charge was a minor in possession, and four counts of an open container. One for each empty beer can. I didn't even try to explain I'd downed but a single Budweiser myself. The cops wouldn't have cared. It was my truck, therefore they were my beers.

Doyle called Rose and she, along with her boss, went to work on my behalf. But the wheels of justice grind slowly, so the charges loomed over my head for several months.

Rose and Doyle continued to date, and while she said yes to dinner, movies, concerts, and a variety of other activities, every night ended with her saying no to more. I was surprised by Doyle's tenacity, but given I had a girlfriend of my own, I didn't spend much time dwelling on my boss's love life.

Clarissa came into the store a few times, and Doyle teased

her some, but for whatever reason kept his lewd comments in check. We even went on a double date once to a concert and dance at the Civic Center. My mom worked there part-time and scored us free entry. Doyle had spent a small fortune wooing Rose, so free was right up his alley.

With both of us attached to girlfriends, Doyle and I seemed to get along better. Several months went by without either of us provoking the other. And then Vail Peterson entered the picture.

Several times a week, a customer would come into Pearl's and ask for products we were either sold out of, or didn't carry at all. Gold Brothers, the store Doyle's dad ran, not only carried more items, but did a much better job of restocking their shelves. So to keep from losing any customers, we called the classier store anytime we couldn't provide the items the clients wanted.

Buck Suggs had hired Vail to help run the register and to take care of their greenhouse. I knew names and voices of all the employees at the other store, but Vail was my favorite. Her voice had a light, airy tone and she had a great laugh. However, I had no idea what she looked like.

I'd seen Doyle's dad, Buck, and Joe, the guy who did their deliveries. I'd even met Kathy, the accountant who handled the books for both stores. But for six months or so, the only contact Vail and I had came via the telephone.

Do y'all have any Terramycin over there?

How many bags of Ferti-Lome do y'all have?

We're out of the gallon-sized root stimulator. Y'all have any?

Hardly deep, thought-provoking conversations, and certainly not life changing. Like everyone else who worked over at Gold Brothers, I assumed Vail to be much older than myself. I never gave much thought to Vail's looks. Then one day she called with a strange request. "Do y'all have any safety pins over there? Buck said there should be some in Pearl's old stuff."

I turned to ask Doyle. "Do we have any safety pins back in your mom's stuff?"

The boss looked up from his recent issue of *Feathered Fury* and asked, "Who wants to know?"

"Vail."

Doyle cocked his head like a curious puppy. "What does she want to know for?

Vail heard him and answered. "My bra strap broke. I need to fix it."

That got Doyle's attention. He closed his magazine, since boobs took precedence over fighting chickens any day. "Yeah, I got a safety pin, but she can only have it if I get to pin it on."

"I'll be right over," Vail answered before I could relay Doyle's message.

I hung up, duly impressed by Doyle's ability to get women to go along with his crazy schemes. Every woman but Rose, it seemed. Fifteen minutes later Vail showed up. Busy trying to explain the best mosquito-killing ratio for mixing Malathion to a customer, I barely caught a glimpse of Vail as she and the boss headed back to his office. Matter of fact, I only caught her backside. She was petite, with shoulder length blonde hair and a nice tight set of buns. The office was still full of artifacts from the dress-making days of the store, so I wasn't surprised to see them head back there for a safety pin.

Ten minutes went by. The customer left with his bottle of pesticide, so I was alone, leaning against the front counter when Vail walked in from the back.

She was pretty. Far prettier than I ever would have imagined. And young. Very near my own age—and extremely well endowed. Given the mission Vail had come for, and the fact she and Doyle had been in the back far longer than it takes to attach a safety pin, my eyes were unable to resist drifting down to her chest.

After months of innocent phone conversation, Vail's first ever words to me face-to-face were, "Ya might as well ask to see 'em if all you're going to do is stand there and stare with your mouth hung open."

I, of course, turned red and mumbled something unintelligible as Vail sashayed out the door. Doyle had quite the laugh at my expense. That in itself was nothing new, but for whatever reason, the episode left me unnerved long after Vail's hasty exit. I had that same hollow feeling down in my gut I got whenever it dawned on me something was about to go terribly wrong. As a kid, the sensation hit me late at night when I realized too late I'd forgotten to do my homework. I'd had that same feeling there in the Bailloux's feed shed when Missy interrupted my escapade with Candy. And the same pain had hit me when that officer asked for my truck keys.

Forgotten obligations. Missed opportunities. Dreaded outcomes. At the time, I wasn't sure which category Vail fit into, but both my gut and I felt the void of her departure. Later, I learned Doyle had orchestrated the whole event. Well, not the whole event. Vail had indeed needed a safety pin, but given Vail's healthy curves, and the tightness of the bright blue blouse she wore that day, the boss knew my eyes would wander. So he'd coached Vail, word for word what to say. And Vail was all too eager to go along with his evil little plan. If only I'd known then how much Vail enjoyed shocking people.

Weeks went by before I gathered the courage to swing by Gold Brothers and apologize to Vail. That apology led to bigger things. Nearly two decades later, I'm forced to smile when I think how a fat, fuzzy-navel-guzzling fool, a long-forgotten safety pin, and a healthy, eye-attracting set of boobs changed my life.

Chapter Twenty-One

Three's a Crowd

When it rains it pours. Clichéd, but true.

I was dating Clarissa when I met and became friends with Vail.

Vail, who would say or do anything and look extremely appealing doing it. Sure, Vail had a boyfriend, a fiancé to be exact, but she made it known a little fun never hurt anyone. And no, I couldn't help but ponder having some of that fun myself.

Then there was Samantha Blake. The girl I'd lusted after most of my school days. Doyle sent me to the bank one day to get change for the store and there she was, on the other side of the glass working as a teller. We talked for a few minutes about old times and common friends, but there were other people in line, so our time was limited.

Samantha was as pretty as ever. As she slid the change through the cubby hole she said, "I wrote my number down for you. Call me sometime. I'd love to hang out."

I nodded and headed back to Pearl's.

Samantha Blake. The very girl I'd been afraid to ask out

for years had given me her number. An open invitation to hang out with her.

Clarissa. Vail. Samantha. All different. All alluring. All claiming a slice of my desire. Don't get me wrong, there are worse problems for a nineteen-year-old male to have, but I was torn. Clarissa was my girlfriend. The only one I'd ever had. Vail was the wildest, craziest girl I'd ever met. I found the promise of excitement she offered quite enticing. And Samantha. Well, hell, how many pages of this story have I devoted to my yearning for Samantha?

Before Rose entered the picture, Doyle would've found a way to juggle all three, had he been in my shoes. Like a circus performer, he embraced death-defying and daring challenges. Flaming chainsaws, ultra-sharp swords, or good-looking women. They were all the same to a man like Doyle. He was unafraid to take risks. To endanger not only himself, but those around him. And up to a point, he was very good at managing such tricks. But I'd witnessed enough in my years at Pearl's to know such feats were impossible to maintain. Eventually the act, the routine, would wear thin and everything would come crashing down.

I didn't want to be Doyle.

I didn't want lose a finger, an eye, or any other appendage.

I didn't want to break any hearts, including my own.

Hell of it was, I still didn't know what I wanted. My boss didn't have that problem. He'd gone from wanting it all, to wanting only one thing.

Rose.

He and the legal secretary had been dating for a number of months, when sometime after Christmas she finally relented and invited him to meet her kids. By mid-March they were taking family picnics to Palo Duro Canyon. Rose, her two kids, and Doyle with his brood of boys. The two clans were even planning a complete family vacation come summer. Possibly to Disneyland.

The mental image of Doyle and his three rough housing boys, floating along to the tune of *It's a Small World After All* amused me, but in the spirit of keeping peace, I kept my sarcastic comments to myself. The question of why my boss was willing to go to so much trouble to bed this one woman was a bigger mystery than why Donald Duck wears a sailor shirt and hat, but no pants.

I was just beginning to think Doyle might actually be in love with Rose, and not merely the challenge she presented, when it happened. Rose invited him to spend the night at her house.

Like everything Rose did, the event was well-planned. Her seven-year-old daughter was going to be away at a slumber party. Her son at his uncle's. Over the months, I'd grown to like Rose. She was smart, funny, and yes, attractive. Of course it didn't hurt that she'd managed to get all of my offenses dropped except the minor in possession. Forty seven dollars and fifty cents later, that charge was taken care of as well. Rose warned me that should I get a second such citation before I turned twenty-one, the judge would most likely hammer me with a fine ten-times that much.

Neither Rose, nor her boss, ever charged me a single cent. After everything was cleared, I liked to tease my boss by saying, "Rose got me off, long before she ever gave you the chance." But with that chance now imminent, Doyle strutted around the store like a conquering hero. Finding himself quite witty, he couldn't resist bragging the entire week before the big sleepover.

"Subpoena hell." He said grabbing his crotch. "Wait until she gets some o' this 'poena."

"Come Friday night, I'll be putting the sex in sexretary."

"She'll be taking dick-tation all night long."

I was torn. For months, I'd listened to Doyle bitch about his shrinking wallet and growing libido. Every morning after one of their dates, he'd whine about her not allowing him to explore her legal briefs. With the return of his cocky swagger and crude comments, I knew it was indeed the challenge he'd been pursuing and not the woman. Afterwards, his desire for Rose would shrivel like the petals of her namesake in a hot August sun. After all her careful patience, Rose would still get hurt.

Then karma intervened. Her daughter came down with strep throat. The whole thing was called off.

Rose was saved.

Doyle was livid. Doubly so when I chimed in with my belief fate had intervened. The boss asked what I meant by that.

I told him.

We argued.

He fired me. Again.

This time I resolved not to go back. I went home. Took a shower, did some homework, and headed over to Clarissa's apartment. Unlike the first time he'd fired me, or the day I'd quit, my sudden unemployment didn't bother me. School was paid for until next fall. I had no rent. I had money enough in the bank to buy gas for my truck until I found something else and most importantly, I didn't have to search for company the way I had before.

Clarissa considered my firing a good thing. "Now you can move to Lubbock with me. And go to Tech in the fall." She was giddy with excitement. Then again, Clarissa was nearly always giddy with excitement.

Job or no job, I wasn't moving to Lubbock. I had sense enough to realize living in the same town as her dad, a man with state-mandated power to pass judgment on others, was not a smart move. And while I liked Clarissa, and enjoyed her company, I wasn't truly in love with her. When exactly that realization had hit me I can't say, but by that time I knew it for a fact. But proving I'd learned more than I cared to admit from Doyle, I didn't bring any of that up. Not then. Not with Clarissa in such a celebratory mood.

I left her apartment somewhere in the neighborhood of four in the morning. I had but one class on Fridays, eight A.M. Freshman Comp II. Five minutes late, I made it to my seat despite the fact I was operating on less than three hours sleep. An hour later I drove away from the campus relieved I didn't have to head into work. A nice fat breakfast burrito and a nap were the only items on my agenda. I'd just inhaled the former and stretched out in preparation for the latter when the phone rang.

I checked the caller I.D. and recognized the number for Gold Brothers. Figuring it was Vail, I went ahead and answered. The caller turned out to be Doyle's dad, Buck.

He knew his son had fired me the day before, but he would consider it a personal favor if I went back to work at Pearl's. He told me Joe and Vail were having to run to store because Doyle hadn't showed up. But Joe needed to make Gold Brother's afternoon deliveries. So I would be doing him a huge favor if I went in and helped Vail. And, he promised me a job for as long as I wanted it, regardless of what Doyle had to say on the matter.

I went, but if I'm telling the truth, I did it more to hang out with Vail than to bail Buck Suggs out of a jam. That, and I wanted to hear the dirt on why Doyle hadn't showed for work. But Vail didn't know. After Joe headed off, leaving us alone, Vail told me no one had heard a word from Doyle. A customer had come into Gold Brothers earlier that morning, saying Pearl's was still closed. An hour later Buck called to see if Pearl's had any pre-emergent left. When no one answered, he sent Joe and Vail over to see what was up.

Doyle had done a lot of things in the years I'd known him,

but not once had he failed to show for work. The prodigal son stumbled in just after one that afternoon. His hair was askew and dark circles rimmed his bloodshot eyes.

Standing in the doorway he looked first at me and then at Vail, before saying, "What the fuck is he doing here?"

"Buck hired him back. He wants you to call him."

"Right after I take a nap." Doyle staggered back to his office.

A little after six, Doyle was still back there with the lights off and the door shut. As agreed upon, Vail and I waited in the parking lot for Buck to swing by and collect the bank deposit.

Handing over the day's earnings, we told Buck his son was passed out in the office. The elder Suggs shook his head and went to confront Doyle.

Vail and I left.

Together.

Her boyfriend had just departed for boot camp, and I decided I'd rather spend the evening with Vail than Clarissa.

Saturday morning, I headed into Pearl's, dreading a confrontation with Doyle. But there was none. Not one word was said about my firing. After I finished taking care of the animals and sweeping the floor, Doyle said, "Thanks for holding down the fort yesterday. Had a rough night. Picked up this gal at the Caravan. Man did we ever get fucked up. Been a long time since I smoked any of that shit. I'm getting too old."

Clarissa called the store shortly after that. Doyle handed me the phone. Whispering, he said, "It's your girlfriend. She sounds pissed."

I hadn't talked to her since I left her apartment early the day before. No doubt she was angry I'd gone AWOL on a Friday night. She would be even more so if I told her I'd spent the time with Vail. It wouldn't matter that Vail and I had done nothing even remotely romantic. I'd helped her write an essay and then spent three hours tutoring her in College Algebra. Her parents fed me dinner, and we watched a rented movie on her couch alongside her mom, dad, and two little brothers. But Clarissa wouldn't care about any of that.

"Hello," I said.

"Where have you been? I called your house last night and your mom said you hadn't come home from work yet. I didn't tell her you'd gotten fired. Good thing, since you obviously lied about that, too."

"I did get fired."

"Yeah, I can tell. That's why you're there now."

"Doyle's dad rehired me."

"And he made you work all night, I suppose?"

"No," I said, dreading the question I knew would come next. "I got off at my usual time."

Rather than ask where I'd gone, or how I'd spent my night, Clarissa surprised me by saying, "You shouldn't have gone back. The semester will be over in a few months and I have plenty of money to get us by until we move to Lubbock. We really should …" Clarissa kept right on talking, but I stopped listening. All those we's and us's made me nervous.

I looked over at Doyle, reclined with his feet propped up on the counter. Despite having had a full night to recuperate, he still looked like hammered dog shit, even with his eyes shut. Crow's feet and other deep lines etched his face. His hair had begun to lighten around the temples. His three-day-old stubble was flecked with gray. I suppose the evidence of his lifestyle had been there for a while, but I'd never noticed how much he'd aged until that moment. I stared at him while Clarissa carried on about Lubbock. I wondered what lies Doyle had told the woman he picked up. What story had made her decide to take him home for the night. Had he promised her a relationship, a future that was never going to happen? For that matter, what had he told Rose? Had she called his house all night, searching for him? Wondering why he wouldn't answer?

"I'm not moving to Lubbock," I said into the receiver. "Not when the semester is over. Not ever."

Silence greeted me.

"Look, Clarissa. I should've told you before now, but I've never planned to go. I can't afford tuition at Tech."

"But we've talked about this for months."

I shook my head, though she couldn't see it. "No. You talked. I listened, and like an idiot never said I wasn't going to go."

For the next fifteen minutes Clarissa tried to change my

mind. She described a future I wasn't interested in. In a city I didn't care to dwell. Doyle opened one eye and stared as I shot down her plans. Normally, he would've reveled in the situation. Chimed in with tips, or popped off a slew of smart-ass comments. Normally, he would have enjoyed my discomfort. But he was still harboring ill-effects from his night of drinking, smoking, and screwing around.

Finally, Clarissa said, "If you aren't interested in going to Lubbock when school is out, then I don't see any reason for us to see each other now."

"Neither do I," I said, and hung up the phone.

Eyes still shut, the boss asked, "Trouble in paradise?"

"Not anymore," I answered.

"You did the right thing. Don't get tied down to one woman. Never fucking works out."

The last thing I wanted to hear was a lecture or life lesson from Doyle. Especially about commitment.

I headed to the back and busied myself restacking tomato cages. The reason all his relationships went to shit had nothing to do with him committing to one woman. Most of the time, it had everything to do with his inability to do so.

I hadn't broken up with Clarissa because I was scared, or running from a long-term relationship. The idea of having exactly that appealed to me. I'd yet to find a person who was truly happy without one.

But Clarissa wasn't who I wanted to spend the rest of my life with. We'd dated long enough for that much to be clear.

The brand of feed we sold at Pearl's was called ACCO, and once a month or so their regional salesman stopped in to plug new products, talk up old ones they didn't think we were pushing hard enough, or to discuss the company's latest promotion.

I was still in the back, jacking around with the tomato cages and avoiding Doyle when the rep showed up. The guy motioned me up front when I looked his direction.

Wearing the cheesy grin of a true salesman, he extended a hand as I approached. "Trevor, right?"

I shook my head. "Travis."

"Dammit," he said, pumping my fist. "I'm horrible with names." He flashed another smile. "You ever recommend Horse and Mule to y'all's customers here at …" His eyes roamed around the room. "… here at … your feed store," he finally said, when he couldn't find any indication of the joint's actual name.

"Sometimes," I answered.

"I was telling your boss here about our newest contest. Starts Monday. Dealer that sells the most Horse and Mule between now and May first wins a four-day cruise out of Galveston. Ever been to Cozumel?"

I shook my head.

"Sun and fun at sea. Lots of good-looking women on those ships and nothing gets them in the mood like an ocean sunset." The man winked and nudged me with an elbow.

When I didn't say anything, he said, "Start pushing

enough Horse and Mule out the door and Doyle here just might take you when the store wins the contest."

"Hell I will," Doyle said. "When I win that contest I ain't about to take another swinging dick with me. Hell, no. When, not if, but WHEN I win, I'm taking Rose." Doyle spent the rest of the afternoon staring at the pamphlet detailing ACCO's gimmick.

The winning dealer and a guest of their choice would receive one room aboard the cruise ship, transportation to and from Galveston, and five hundred dollars spending money.

The gentle sway of the ocean. Sunsets over the water. All the mixed drinks you want. Beautiful white sand beaches. Crystal blue waters. Doyle read the printed hype aloud. Then he created some of his own.

No depositions. No sick kids. No outside interference.

Rose couldn't deny him under those conditions. Our store had never won so much as a secondary prize in any of ACCO's quarterly contests, but I recognized that look in Doyle's eye. He aimed to win. Regardless of the cost.

Chapter Twenty-Two

The Big Door Prize

Horse and Mule, the product featured in the cruise contest, was a multi-animal sweet-grain. The fifty pound bags contained steam rolled oats, corn, and barley, all bound together with molasses. Despite being called "horse and mule" it could be fed to goats, sheep, and cattle, as well as all types of equine.

In order to move more bags of Horse and Mule, Doyle stopped ordering every other type of horse feed. Telling the customers the higher-end products were on back order, he talked people with hogs, cows, and goats into buying the stuff. He was a hell of a salesman. To insure he'd win, Doyle ordered an extra thirty tons of the stuff and stored it in the freight car where we normally kept hay.

The short part of the story is that he won the trip and Rose agreed to go.

Doyle's word was filled with sunshine and lollipops. Figuring he'd hit upon a sure thing, the boss made excuses to cancel and postpone dates with Rose. Why spend money on her, when the cruise was only three weeks away?

Doyle and Rose were to depart the week before Vail's fiancé was to finish boot camp. He would only be home a short time before heading back for technical training; nevertheless I wasn't looking forward to her boyfriend's return, as Vail and I had begun spending all of our free hours together.

More often than not we were at her house. In her room. Mostly, but not entirely, hunched over college textbooks, working on her homework.

Vail was not a strong student. A year younger than me, she'd earned enough high school credits to graduate mid-year. In a hurry for independence, she'd jumped straight into college courses at Amarillo College, but the pace was giving her fits. Classes were not the only thing dogging Vail. Her parents didn't like her fiancé.

They did like me. And they never missed an opportunity to voice those opinions. After the animosity from Clarissa's father, I welcomed their approval, though I couldn't quite figure out Vail's take on the matter. Her parents rode her hard, pushing, suggesting, informing her of the correct way, their way, to do everything. Vail was rebellious, and the more they pressed the less likely she was to listen. Yet, at least where I was concerned, she seemed inclined to agree with her parents.

"You would be better for me than Jimmy," she said one evening.

Her mom had just poked her head into Vail's room and said, "Too bad that other boy was never smart enough to help you like Travis does."

"That other boy." That's what both her mom and dad called him. And at times, Vail acted as if she'd dismissed him. too. Then, out of the blue she'd say, "I can't wait until Jimmy gets back." One day her finger would be adorned with the ring he'd bought her, the next the gold band and tiny diamond would be nowhere in sight.

Mixed signals, mixed actions, and my mixed-up feelings made for some strange evenings. Adding to my confusion was the fact I regularly volunteered to make the bank runs for Doyle. Making certain to wind up at Samantha Blake's window, I'd sometimes let half a dozen other customers go ahead, just to ensure those precious few minutes in her presence.

I kept the slip of paper where she'd written her phone number neatly folded inside my wallet. I'd gotten it out a few times and contemplated dialing Samantha up, but never managed to actually carry the task through.

Why?

I can't rightly say. Not even now, nearly two decades after the fact. Was it residual school boy fear? From the days when even a simple conversation with Samantha left my palms sweaty and my heart thumping wildly? Was it confusion over Vail? Was it concern that the fantasy of dating Samantha would outshine the reality? A combination of all the above, I suspect.

Then, the day before Doyle was scheduled to hit the high seas, Samantha slid the store's change bag across the granite countertop. When I reached for it, she placed her hand on mine. "Are you ever going to get around to asking me out?"

I stared into her eyes, swallowed the lump in the throat and said, "I've been thinking about it. But I was kind of waiting until I was rich and famous, so you wouldn't be able to say no."

Our eyes held. The heat from her fingertips warmed my hand. "I'm not going to say no."

"How about next Friday? A week from today."

She smiled and pulled her hand away. "Okay, but only if you promise to call me before then." Staring over my shoulder, she called out, "Next!" A man in a dark business suit took my place at the teller window.

It's hard to say who was more excited that afternoon, Doyle or myself. The boss talked non-stop about the cruise. About the things he was going to do with, and to, Rose. About the pictures he was gonna bring back to verify his prowess.

Focused on my impending date with Samantha, his arrogance didn't bother me the way it might have otherwise. I already had plans with Vail for both that night and the next, which is why I'd asked Samantha out the following weekend. Now that I had set plans with Samantha Blake, the confusion I felt over Vail had lifted.

We were meant to be friends. Nothing more. I was sure of it.

Besides, I told myself. Her fiancé was coming home in ten

days. It was in everybody's best interest for me to concentrate on Samantha. I toyed with the idea of canceling my plans with Vail. Of calling up Samantha and moving up our date, but I'd already waited years. What was one more week?

Chapter Twenty-Three

The Offer At Hand

Doyle hired a guy to help me run the store while he was off sailing the high seas with Rose. A guy named Ricky Bonds.

Ricky was a long standing customer at the store. He and his wife owned a landscaping business and they bought most of their supplies from us. The happy little landscaping couple claimed to be youth ministers at their church. And I don't doubt they were, but my gut told me their righteousness ran only skin deep.

Ricky and his wife were in their mid-twenties. Only five or six years older than me, but I felt very little connection with them.

They were religious zealots.

The kind that never let an opportunity to plug their faith or church slip by, but their repeated sales speeches wore thin for me. Especially given the fact I didn't believe they were half as wholesome as they let on.

She was a skinny little blonde who favored black lacy bras covered by blouses with gaping necklines. I know this because she would come into the store and lean on the counter, exposing her undergarments and the tops of her milky white breasts. She wasn't particular about who stood on the opposite side of the counter.

One could argue it was the boss's and my morals, not hers, in question. After all, we were the ones gazing upon the forbidden apples, but on more than one occasion I managed to shift my eyes upward, only to find Ricky's wife smiling mischievously back at me. I can't say for certain she wanted someone to take a bite of her offered fruit, but I do know she reveled in the attention.

That brings us to Ricky. He struck me as a bicycle seat sniffer, a closet pervert, just waiting for a chance to display his depraved side. He didn't disappoint me, though it took longer for the truth to come out than I first imagined. Ricky Bonds was a model citizen the four days I worked with him. Then again, my mind wasn't exactly focused at the time.

In a calculated move, I first called Samantha on Sunday afternoon. I didn't want to appear too eager by calling the very night she'd told me to, or even the next day, so I figured Sunday, two days after the fact, was about right. Samantha told me she liked to dance so I told her about a local rodeo coming up on Friday. A concert and dance was to follow the last event. She said it sounded like fun.

Monday she called me, and we again talked for better than an hour. I learned she too had recently broken off a long-term relationship. Looking back, I find it humorous the things my nineteen-year-old mind considered long-term, like the four and a half months I dated Clarissa.

Samantha and I talked again on Tuesday and Wednesday. But not Thursday, the day before our date. I tried to call her, even left a message, to no avail.

Doyle and Rose flew back to Amarillo that day, and late in the afternoon the boss came shuffling in, looking more like a Titanic survivor than any of the happy vacationers I'd seen in ACCO's glossy brochure.

Rose wasn't with him, so Ricky looked eagerly at the boss. "Let's see the pictures."

Doyle shook his head. "Ain't no damned pictures." The boss didn't want to tell us the truth, but Ricky and I bugged, badgered, and buffaloed him until he begrudgingly relayed the details of his trip.

Karma, in the form of Rose's sick daughter, had bitten Doyle in the ass the first time he'd thought the prize was in the bag. Aboard the ship it had been Mother Nature's turn to take a chunk out of his hide.

Doyle had few scruples, especially those governing little Doyle, but as he put it, "I ain't the kind of guy who likes to swim the red tide."

According to our boss, the crew no more than raised the ship's gangplank when Rose received her monthly visitor. They'd gotten in a huge argument when he accused her of knowing she was gonna be on the rag. She assured him the visit was early. That she thought it would be okay until maybe the last day.

Doyle admitted to losing his mind. He said they barely spoke the rest of that day.

"What about the sunset?" I asked. "I thought those at-sea sunsets put everybody in the mood?"

Doyle ignored my sarcasm. "I went to the casino and got drunk. I don't know what the fuck Rose did, but she woke me up early the next morning."

"And?" Ricky was wide-eyed with anticipation.

"A fucking hand job." Doyle shook his head. "She gave me a fucking hand job. Expected that to make up for everything. You know how much damn money I've spent on her these last six months?"

I bit my lip and tried not to laugh.

"I have thirty fucking tons of Horse and Mule stockpiled in my hay trailer, and she thinks jacking me off makes up for six-grand worth of grain."

"I deserved a blow job at the very least. But did I get one? Hell, no!" Now that the boss had gotten riled up, he paced around like a televangelist delivering hell-fire and brimstone.

"Oh, I probably could have talked her into it, but to top everything else, she got a damned fever blister on her upper lip. Claimed it was from the stress. Tried to blame her damn herpes on me yelling at her. But I ain't stupid. I know fucking herpes when I see it. Last thing I wanted was her giving me that shit." Doyle collapsed into a chair.

"You can get herpes from a fever blister?" Ricky asked.

Doyle frowned at his newest employee.

I enjoyed seeing him give that look to someone other than me.

"You're kidding me," the boss said. "Where the hell you been, Ricky? Fever blisters ARE herpes, and the last thing I want is a giant scab on the end of my dick."

That's when I lost it. The irony of Doyle's woeful tale, combined with the shocked and disgusted expression on Ricky's face was more than I could take. Neither Ricky nor Doyle joined me, but I laughed until tears came down.

My mirth didn't last long. One day, to be exact. I can't remember the exact story she gave.

My cousin came into town.

I have to shampoo my hair.

My dog has fleas.

Pick whichever bullshit line you like best. The facts remain the same. Samantha Blake blew me off. Not in the manner Doyle wanted Rose to blow him off, but in the manner of ... *I don't want to jeopardize our friendship by complicating our relationship.*

She drove a dagger through my heart. She canceled our date. Mere hours before it had a chance to happen. The date I'd waited years for. The date for which I'd looked into her eyes and heard her say, "I won't say no."

When I asked about Saturday night or the next week, Samantha said, "Look, Travis. You are a great guy and I cherish our friendship, but it's not a good time for me. I'll call you later in the week."

I hung up the phone.

It rang almost immediately.

I yanked it up, hoping it was Samantha. Maybe she'd changed her mind a second time.

"Hello?" I said.

"Travis?"

Expecting to hear Samantha, it took me a second to recognize Vail's voice.

"Did I dial Pearl's number?"

"Yeah, sorry. I meant to say 'feed store' but I was thinking about something else."

Vail laughed.

God, I loved her laugh.

"Hey," she said. "Go outside or do something away from the phone. I want Doyle to answer so I can pretend to be a customer. I wanna ask him if he has any Horse and Mule."

I'd called Vial the previous night to tell her about Doyle's cruise. We'd had quite the laugh at his expense. I'd found it easier to talk to Vail once I realized my feelings for her were more about friendship than anything else.

"Okay," I said. "But what are you doing tonight?"

"Nothing," she said. "I spent all my money on first and last month's rent. I'm broke until Jimmy gets to town on Monday."

"I have an extra ticket for tonight. You wanna go?"

"What happened to your date?"

"She bailed on me."

"Not Samantha Blake, the fairest maiden in all the land," Vail teased.

"You wanna go or not?"

Vail laughed. This time I didn't find the sound quite as melodious. "Yeah, I'll go, but don't get your testicles twisted in a knot just because your wet dreams aren't going to come true. Though I do have to point out, that's what you get for making fun of Doyle. He lost the chance to bang his dream girl and now, so have you."

"Maybe, but you made fun of him too. What if Jimmy decides to marry some G.I. Jane instead of you?"

"Who said Jimmy was my dream guy?"

"You did," I pointed out. "When you said yes and put on his ring."

"Yeah, well, sometimes a girl has to take the offer at hand. If she wants to better herself."

Already feeling like I'd been kicked in the nuts, my conversation with Vail did little to lift my spirits. I cringed at the idea life was about taking the offer at hand, but as the afternoon wore on I couldn't help but wonder if Vail was right. Maybe I was wrong. Maybe I'd read too many books, watched too many movies. Maybe love and happiness were nothing more than a blind wager. Like betting on black or red on a roulette wheel. Of course, the odds were actually longer than that. Maybe they were too long. Maybe that's why so many people were willing to settle for the offer at hand.

Chapter Twenty-Four

Hold On It's A Bumpy Ride

Later that night, I picked up Vail at her new apartment, and away we went. For a couple of hours we watched skinny little cowboys, they no doubt prefer the term wirey, get bucked off a variety of animals.

When the competition ended, the crowd made their way down from the stands to the dirt-covered arena. Well, it was mostly dirt. Given the fact the arena had seen many a hoof that night, there also happened to be a tidy amount of organic matter mixed with the soil. After a bit the lights dimmed, perhaps so we wouldn't know what we were dancing in, and the band kicked off. I'm not the world's best dancer and never have been, but I can two-step well enough to get by.

Vail and I danced a few songs and then she said, "Hey, there's Jennifer Kellogg."

I glanced the direction Vail pointed, more to be polite than anything else. I knew the name, Jennifer Kellogg, and my opinion of the girl associated with it was not all that good.

Once upon a time, Jennifer Kellogg had been Hunter Tomkins' girlfriend. You may recall Hunter as the guy I stole my job from at Pearl's. I'd seen her around with him, but had never actually talked to her. Looking over at her now, I took in her long blonde hair, and bright smile. I begrudgingly acknowledged the fact she was pretty, but I couldn't help wonder why a girl like her would want anything to do with an idiot like Hunter Tomkins.

"You know her?" Vail asked.

I shrugged. "Sort of, but she's kind of a snob."

Vail frowned. "No, she's not. Jennifer is super nice. She's a year younger than me, but we had a few classes together in high school. I'm gonna go talk to her." Off Vail went, leaving me alone on the dance floor.

While she was away I stopped to talk to some other friends I knew. I was still standing there when I felt a tap on my shoulder. Turning around, I found myself staring into the green eyes of the aforementioned Jennifer Kellogg.

"I am NOT a snob," she said.

I looked passed Jennifer at Vail's smiling face. I wasn't the least bit surprised my friend had gone straight over and told on me. Like Doyle, Vail enjoyed seeing other's people worm their way out of awkward situations.

"Why would you say that about me?" Jennifer demanded.

The old Travis, the one who existed before years of torment and booby-trapped situations at the hands of Doyle Suggs, would have quickly apologized and fled. But I'd learned to cope with such situations. I'd learned to stand my ground and play it out.

"Well," I said. "I used to see you around when you were dating Hunter Tomkins. And not once did you ever speak to me."

Jennifer smiled. "That's probably because I figured you were an asshole."

"Why would you think that?"

Pushing back a strand of her blond hair, Jennifer said, "Hunter was an asshole and so were his friends."

"Me and him," I shook my head, "we were never friends. So that makes me …" I paused to smile. "Not an asshole," I answered.

"I know. Vail told me. That's why I came over here to dance with you."

I danced with Jennifer to nearly every song from that point on. She gave me her number, and a brilliant smile, when I asked. She was lighter on her feet and a better dancer than me, despite the fact she repeatedly tried to lead.

I, of course, let her, because of the way her hand felt in mine.

Vail didn't mind the fact I'd ditched her as a dance partner. Turns out Jennifer had gone to the rodeo with some guy both of them knew, and Vail partnered up with him. He was no doubt a better dancer than me so we both made out. No one stepped on Vail's toes, and I got to spend the night getting to know Jennifer.

"Funny, isn't it," Vail said as we drove back to her apartment.

"What?"

"How you can go from thinking someone is a bitch and a snob one second, to enthralling the next."

"I never said she was a bitch," I answered.

"True, but you were thinking it, and now you're thinking about other things."

I pulled up at Vail's apartment complex. "She seems fun," I admitted. "I'll call her."

"You better," Vail said. "Because, I told her you would."

I turned off the truck. Vail sat staring up at her door on the second floor of the complex. "I hate coming home to an empty place."

I shrugged. "Jimmy will be back in two days."

"Yeah, but then he leaves again."

Neither of us said anything for a nearly a minute then, Vail turned to me, "You could come up, you know. Stay for a while. Even the night, if you want. That way neither of us would have to go home alone."

I knew what Vail was saying, offering. But getting out and going upstairs with her wasn't really what I wanted. I'm not gonna lie and say there weren't parts of me that wanted to, but not my brain. Not my heart. I truly did have higher aspirations than taking the offer at hand.

"I better not," I finally said.

Smiling, Vail said, "I didn't think you would. That's why I like you." She leaned over, kissed me on the cheek, and climbed out of my truck. Halfway to her door, she turned around and yelled back, "Call Jennifer. Y'all would make a great couple."

Vail said the exact same thing four-and-a-half years later. At the rehearsal dinner. The night before Jennifer and I said our "I do's." That was nineteen years ago, but I'm getting ahead of myself.

I left Pearl's not long after that night. Right about the same time Vail and Jimmy headed down to the Justice of the Peace and tied the knot.

Vail quit one day. Me the next. The two were not related, not exactly anyway. Since she was heading off to Kansas to play housewife on some Army base, and I was leaving to take a job at the post office. My stamp-licking gig was only supposed to last a hundred and eighty days but it paid better than double my salary at Pearl's. Besides, I was ready for a change.

I gave Doyle two weeks' notice, but he cut me loose the very same day, saying, "Fuck Travis. If you stick around here I'll be tempted to jack with you one last time. One or both of us will end up pissed and you'll go away hating both me and this place. We've had too much fun over the years for that to happen."

Doyle, of course, was right. When I look back at those days, I do so with a tinge of nostalgia, but at the time I emerged from the feed store feeling like I'd survived some sort of natural disaster. I imagined myself staggering forward with matted hair and streaks of dirt across my face. Sort of like a rescued coal miner, freed after spending days below ground.

Some might say that description is a bit dramatic but I can present the fate of one Ricky Bonds as evidence otherwise. Ricky was the lawn mowing youth minister who took Doyle's place while he was off sailing the red sea with Rose. Ricky was also my replacement when I left the feed store. Ricky took the job with a wife, a respectable position of standing within his church, and all of his hair.

His downward spiral began with the occasional happy hour after work, for you see, Ricky was one thing I never was to Doyle—a friend and coworker of legal drinking age. The happy hours soon turned into late nights at the honkytonks. Not three months after going to work full-time for Doyle, Ricky Bonds found a girlfriend on the side. Then that girlfriend found his wife and Ricky was out both a wife and Sunday job at his church.

About the same time his ex-wife found somebody new to stare at her cleavage, Ricky found his first DUI. Ricky married some gal he picked up at the bar. That relationship lasted only until she maxed out all his credit cards and split for parts unknown.

Two years after I left Pearl's, Doyle followed suit and quit to take a job with benefits and a nice 401k. Ricky stayed behind to run the store.

Pearl's has long since closed. Buck retired and shut down both joints in order to spend his days panning for gold up in

Colorado. Five or six years ago I ran into Ricky Bonds. Jennifer and I had gone out to a local bar to see Willie Nelson perform, and even though I didn't recognize him at first, there was Ricky, minus the permed mullet that once served as his 'do of choice. Actually, the long permed hair in the back was still there, but the top of his head was slicker than one of Doyle's pick-up lines.

I talked to Ricky for a few minutes, and as Jennifer and I walked away, he called out, "Hey, ya'll come back next Friday if you get the chance. First beer is on me. I'm here most nights."

I'd like to think that wouldn't have been me. That I would've had the strength to not become that guy, heading to the bar every night. That guy desperately trying to hang onto the fleeting time in his life when someone, anyone, thought he was cool.

Ricky is still trapped down there, living in that dark, cold shaft. Just hoping the canary doesn't die, but me, I was rescued.

By Vail, that night she orchestrated my exchange with Jennifer.

By Doyle, in more ways than I could ever count.

And of course, by Jennifer.

Schoolboy crushes, lustful encounters, misguided relationships. They make for easy writing, but love, at least true love, is quite difficult to describe. I suppose a better writer would wax poetically about pitter-pattering hearts, sleepless nights, and overwrought emotions, but I warned you in the beginning that this coming-of-age story isn't fraught with symbolism, hidden metaphors, or heaping mounds of other literary devices. Nope, this story is about love, life, and happiness. This story is as much about tomorrow as it is yesterday, for I have few regrets in life. Least of all the two things I stole from Hunter Tomkins—the opportunity to work for Doyle Suggs at Pearl's Feed and Seed, and the woman Hunter let slip from his grasp.

    I suppose we all wish for things from time to time. I know I do. And I'm thankful for the blessings that have came my way, but without a doubt, the best thing to ever happen to me came not from a fulfilled wish, but from one that was not. For that I have to thank Samantha Blake. The girl who blew me—off, that is.

    Someone, perhaps even Doyle, could've warned me about the unexpected twists and turns fate dishes out, but I'm glad they didn't. Life wouldn't be nearly as much fun that way.

Where Are They Now?

Darlene Wilshire—My very first date is married and ironically now lives in Arkansas, where, at least according to Doyle, a woman with that name needs to dwell. She is married with children, but I do wonder if she ever thinks of me when she sees peonies in bloom.

Cody Hawkins—Is angry because I refuse to be his Facebook friend. He asks and sends me messages about once a month, but the memory of that cue ball hitting me upside the head is still a bit too fresh for me to give a shit even two decades later.

John Bailloux—Never left Amarillo. His lip has been permanently disfigured by years of cramming it full of Copenhagen. He remains a nice guy with simple expectations. As a result, he is perhaps the happiest person I know.

Candy Bailloux—To my knowledge has never returned to Amarillo or married. I do not believe she has any chickens to feed either, which is a real shame as she had quite a talent for it.

Missy Bailloux—John and Candy's little sister graduated high school with honors. Moved away to college and is now a vice president in some sort of Aviation Company. Like her siblings, she has never married, but something tells me she still reads Harlequin romances, dreaming of the day a cowboy with a white hat will gallop in and swoop her up to ride off into the sunset. But I bet there ain't no chickens on that ranch.

Steve Golds—Whose baseball dreams were derailed by the unexpected arrival of his first child, is now married with two sons better than a decade younger than his daughter. He coaches their Little League teams, and despite never becoming a baseball star, he seems to be thriving.

Brent and Lisa—Are still married but by all accounts are miserable. They have a brood of kids, a heard of hounds, and not much else. I've seen him a dozen or so times over the years but not once has he been close to sober.

Scott—It pains me that I understated Scott's role as my friend in this book, but while he was always there, in the circle of people in my life, he somehow managed to avoid getting caught up in the more circus-like events, which is why he isn't mentioned much in this text. However, there is one Scott incident of note.

For most of our high school days he dated a girl named Jennifer. No, not the same one I went on to marry. We all took it for granted that Scott and Jennifer would eventually get hitched, and in a fit of insanity he decided one day I should use my rabbit tattooer to permanently ink the first three letters of her name upon his shoulder. Show rabbits must have an identifying tattoo in their ear and I owned the equipment to do so. On the scale of art, these tattoos ranked well below prison tats, but Scott wanted JEN on his arm, so I arranged the needlelike tiles and pushed them through his skin. I rubbed Indian ink in afterwards and suddenly Scott's arm read JEN. His Jennifer ditched him the next week. Distraught, Scott downed a case of Coor's Light and reached for a belt sander. It took weeks for the scab to heal and when it did he had a large scar that covered most of his shoulder. The letters JEN remained visible, though the sanding did lighten the color. A year later, against every last one of his friend's advice, he married an entirely different girl named Jennifer. They divorced. Scott finally gave up on Jennifers and found happiness by marrying my cousin.

Samantha Blake—Samantha is still beautiful on the outside. She married a wealthy, wealthy man of some importance locally. I see her about town occasionally, and we speak, but her spirit seems to have broken. It's been years since I've seen her smile and her eyes no longer glisten. Friends tell me she and her husband have little to do with each other beyond public appearances.

Jerry Greer—Since the 'fight that wasn't' between me and Jerry, which Doyle instigated with the rooster/capon encounter, Jerry Greer was never seen or heard from again. Though I'm sure he will one day return to give me the lesson I so badly deserve.

Hopalong—Raced a train to an intersection. The train won.

Rusty the Cable Guy—Still works for the cable company, and I have no doubt still sits somewhere for hours on end while impatient customers wait for sometime between 10 am and 2 pm to arrive.

Pro Wrestler Dirty Dick Murdoch—Died in 1996 of a heart attack.

Pro Wrestler Terry Funk—Continues to be involved in professional wrestling, as well as act. He is nearing 70, can barely walk due to knee damage, and yet, the day he took a stationary bike next to me at the gym, the Funkster rode faster, farther, and at a higher degree of difficulty than I ever could.

Jimmy Bluejacket—Should be out of prison by now, but then again he never was the brightest guy around.

Tasha—Will no doubt be first in line to buy a hundred copies of this book seeing how she loved me so. Just so you know Tasha, bring cash, because I'm not trading it out.

Ginger—Married, but never had children. She painted up until a few years ago but seemingly has retired, as I have not heard of her work being displayed anywhere for a while now. But I know she never got over Wagner's unfortunate and untimely death.

Wagner—Sure was tasty.

Delinda and Darcy Marie—Are no doubt out there somewhere over the rainbow, but I have no idea where.

Rose—I was watching the local news a number of years after my days at Pearl's. There was Rose, talking about her platform and ideals. She had a different last name, so obviously she'd remarried. She was running for city commissioner in the upcoming election. She lost by a wide margin and never again have I seen or heard a word about her, but I suppose she still lives and works here in Amarillo.

Hong—Went to prison for bookmaking, drug dealing, and conspiracy to commit murder, further proving … I'm lucky to be alive.

Clarissa Cates—As planned, Clarissa moved to Lubbock. She called me shortly thereafter and told me she was pregnant. I would have been worried except her cousin had already called and warned me that Clarissa was going to fake being pregnant to try and get me to move to Lubbock. I didn't tell my former girlfriend I'd been tipped off. Instead I remained calm and said, "Let me know when your next doctor's appointment is and I'll drive down and go with you." I never heard from her again.

Vail—I wish I could say life has worked out well for Vail. Sadly it has not. A couple of divorces. A stint in jail. Another in rehab. Turns out the offer at hand does not always lead to good things or happiness.

But I don't want your last thought of Vail to be about such serious matters, so I'm gonna tell you another Vail tale. When Jennifer and I married we bought a house and some property in the country that sat alongside a creek. The water in that creek wasn't the cleanest around, given that a number of large cattle feedlots lined the area upstream. One night, after a bit of alcohol induced revelry, Vail and my friend Scott decided they would go skinny dipping in the creek. And so they did. But Vail had gotten her belly button pierced the day before and a few days later it became infected. She had to remove the stud when her gut began to look like an overripe, pus-oozing eggplant.

To this day I have never seen anything grosser than Vail's infected naval. Yeah, that is a much better thought to end with. Thanks for asking.

Hunter Tomkins—I ran into Hunter at a hardware store maybe a year back. Skinny, bowlegged, and drunk best describes his condition on that day. I listened and tried to avoid the odor of his polluted breath as he told me about his job as a working cowboy on a big ranch south of Amarillo.

Ricky Bonds—Will buy you a beer if you ever find yourself at Midnight Rodeo. Because, he is there most every Friday night.

Austin Suggs—I was about halfway through writing The Feedstore Chronicles when a young man approached me at the grocery store. "Travis?" he said with uncertainty in his voice. "Yeah," I answered, squinting to put a name with the familiar figure. He was sporting a full bushy beard, but I recognized something familiar about his eyes. "Do you remember me?" he asked? "Austin. Suggs." He stood for a few minutes and told me he was recently divorced and going through a custody battle, but he'd just gotten accepted into fire academy. I tried to mesh the adult man with the skinny boy I'd known, but had a hard time doing so.

Dallas and Houston Suggs—I have not seen either of Doyle's youngest boys since leaving the feed store. I hear they both live in Amarillo and have kids of their own.

Pamela. Doyle's wife #1 & #4—Doyle and Pamela remarried a second time shortly after I left Pearl's. Their second try fared no better than Doyle and Laura's two attempts, but it did keep Doyle from paying child support while it lasted.

Laura. Doyle's wife #2 & #3—Went back to her small hometown, married, and now teaches high school in Oklahoma.

Snuggles—Was stolen from the feed store not long after weaning her litter of mutts. Doyle always claimed to know nothing of her whereabout, but years later I discovered Doyle had handed the bulldog over to Laura as payment to keep quiet about something he didn't want to get out. With Doyle, I hate to guess. Snuggles lived to the ripe old age of fourteen, which is ninety eight in dog years, being doted on and fussed over by Laura. It turns out that Snuggles was one of the few females in this story that got the happy ending she was after all along.

Buck Suggs—Wal-Mart, Lowes and other giant retailers put Buck and Gold Brothers out of business, but Buck had socked away enough money to enjoy his retirement. He spends several months a year panning for gold in Colorado.

Pearl's—Pearl's closed a couple of years after I departed, and six months after Doyle took a job at Haliburton. He was later fired for having an affair with either his boss's wife or daughter. I've heard two different versions of the story, but knowing Doyle, they're both true.

Doyle—Remarried wife number one but divorced her again a few years later. After four marriages to only two women, he tied the knot for a fifth time to a girl a decade and a half younger than himself. By all accounts they are a happy couple in love. Doyle drives a truck.

I tried to get in touch with him to discuss this project, but despite several people giving him my number he has never called. I hear he turned pale upon the news that I was writing about my days at the feed store. Don't worry, Doyle, I left out the really bad stuff. Reliable sources tell me Doyle is born again. A new man devoted to his family and God. Perhaps they are right, but me, I'd have to spend a long weekend with him in Vegas before I was convinced.

Me—Like I said, I left Pearl's shortly after Doyle's doomed cruise. That supposed temporary job with the United States Postal Service has turned into eighteen years of me getting up each morning through rain, sleet or snow to trudge off to our local mail facility. Not once have I ever been fired or felt the need to quit, though I have lots of stories about my colorful, and at times, disgruntled, brethren. Perhaps one day I will write a book and title it the Postal Parables.

Jennifer—This book was about my coming of age, about me finding my place in this world. For over twenty years that place was alongside Jennifer. Various editors and critique partners wanted me to explore my feelings for Jennifer more, but to do so would have increased this book's length and changed the tone. So instead, I concentrated on the many pitfalls and roadblocks I encountered on my journey. Frankly, because that stuff makes for better humor. Jennifer and I laughed together for over two decades. Nearly nineteen of those years as husband and wife, but then the roadblocks and pitfalls caught up to us. Our legacy lives on in two wonderful sons.

*PLEASE READ THE
OPENING CHAPTER OF
TRAVIS'S UPCOMING NOVEL*
...
**WAITING ON
THE RIVER**
*FOUND AT THE BACK OF
THIS BOOK.*

About the Author

TRAVIS ERWIN lives in Texas. His novels include *Twisted Roads* and the upcoming *Waiting on the River*. His writing has also appeared in *Underground Voices*, *Beat to a Pulp*, and *Opium Magazine*. His humorous short story "Plundered Booty" is available as part of the *Deadly By The Dozen* e-anthology, and a trio of Travis's more serious stories make up an e-collection entitled *Whispers*. When not writing, you might find Travis knee-deep in a trout stream, bellying up to a side of beef, or with his elbows firmly planted upon the green felt of a poker table.

To leave Travis a comment, or to learn more about him or *The Feedstore Chronicles* please visit:

- http://www.facebook.com/TheFeedstoreChronicles
- http://www.traviserwin.com/
- http://twitter.com @traviserwin

Acknowledgements

Trust me when I say it takes a team of folks supporting, cheering, and assisting any and every writer. I'm certainly no expectation, and as embarrassing and frightening as my days at the feed store were, I'm even more fearful I've left deserving names off this list. My apologies to those I did.

One of my greatest worries in writing this book was that I'd vilify the man I worked for. I borrowed more than a few things from his many character traits, and yes I often wanted to strangle him, but to my former boss I want to say, thanks for the job, for the friendship, and most importantly, for the life lessons.

To my mom. I have much to thank you for, including my love of books and literature. No doubt the contents of this book have made you now question that gift, but really mom, none of this stuff happened. I swear it didn't.

To my boys Tarek and Zalen. Know I love you, but if I catch you reading THIS book anytime soon you're both grounded.

Critique groups are a writer's family, counselors, and cheering squad. I've been in both bad and good groups, but my critic gang at the time I was creating *The Feedstore Chronicles* was the best I've ever been a part of. Yes, I am talking to you Vicki Schoen, Lisa Pawlowski, Caron Guillo, and Val Conrad.

A core group of friends served as both beta readers, and because I'm as much oral storyteller as writer, listeners, over the years. Truthfully these folks believed in my talents before anyone else. Kathy Lundberg, Andy Reyna, Steve Austin, Kim Sage, Aaron "It Tastes Like Dirt" Sage, El Tigre Loco, Nic "Dolly Llam" Brown , Larry and JaNice Smith, Kim Page, Allan Barrett, Kim Francis, Sandy Carlile, and the world's most fervent Kid Rock fan, Arlene Tellman.

This book would never have been published in the first place without the patience, persistence, and faith of its original publishers, TAG Publishing's Dee Burks, and Liz Ragland.

Jennifer Archer your comments made this book better and your encouragement has kept me going more than once. You are certainly one of my heroes, but hummus? Really?

This latest edition owes a debt to the editing genius of Janna Leadbetter. The mistakes that remain are mine, as are the questionable grammar choices. So should you require writing services of any kind, look up Janna at www.facebook.com/writerjannadonn/

Also look for the audio version of *The Feedstore Chronicles* which would not have be possible without the talent, equipment, and most importantly the patience of its producer Wayne Hughes. Wayne much thanks for letting me invade your soundbooth to create this book in my own voice.

Much thanks to Alex Keto for the cover photo, my son for the back photo and to Loudmouth Designs for the layout. Also to Keith Snyder for the pateince and help he provided.

Last but not least, yeah it's cliché but if you've read this far surely I can get away with one, especially when it is true. I wish to thank the wonderful community of people I encounter every day via the world wide web. *The Feedstore Chronicles* began as a series of posts on my blog and to those who took the time to read and comment on the original posts, this book is dedicated to you, for without that support and positive reinforcement I never would've had the courage to turn those fragmented vignettes into a full length book. Blogging, Facebooking, and Tweeting has brought me into contact with a wide array of amazing people. I'm proud to say my following of regulars is large enough I cannot name y'all individually, but you know who you are.

And a special thank you to the stupendously awesome and talented Stephen Parrish and Erica Orloff for not only believing in me as a writer, but as a friend.

Special Sneak preview of
Travis Erwin's upcoming novel
Available Christmas 2016

Waiting On The River

Chapter 1

Darkness fell early this time of year, and with it came both relief and a resolute comfort. For her it was not unlike the feeling of being tucked carefully into bed after a long, hard day. The cover of darkness meant this, her little corner of earth, was hidden away. Out of the spotlight. Logic told her Eagle's Rest, Idaho, was about as far from the spotlight as she could get, be it day or night. But Lindsay Parker struggled to relax no matter where she called home this month.

She scrutinized not only the faces that stopped in at the Talon Cafe for a bite to eat, but also the license-plates of every strange car passing through. The latter being a new habit she picked up after coming here. Back in Seattle she would've gone crazy trying to maintain such a vigil. The remoteness here in Eastern Idaho held advantages, but she couldn't get too careless. Because here, there was no way to fade away into the busy throng of city-life if someone came nosing around. Here, she was vulnerable in ways she'd never been. But here, she also felt a burgeoning hope, long absent in her travels. Here, she was an actual part of something, not just another nameless faceless person in the crowd.

In Eagle's Rest she was not a stranger, and neither was anyone else. That combination made for all kinds of terrifying possibilities.

Her perch in the passenger seat of Cody's Jeep, afforded her a view of a good portion of the town as it lay along five or six blocks of Idaho State Highway 32, highway in name only. Ray Everham's blue heeler loped across the road, disappearing into the shadows beyond the glow of the town's sparse streetlights. The dog was only one of several that had the run of the town. On this Wednesday evening, there didn't appear to be a person, a vehicle, so much as a stray pooch out of place.

The plastic windows on Cody's CJ-7 did a poor job holding out the November chill, but Lindsay didn't mind. She liked the cold and was glad fall had given way to winter. Yet another thing that came early here, in the shadow of the Tetons, where dates on calendars didn't matter nearly as much as the arctic winds.

Outside the Jeep, Cody rubbed his gloved hands together and cupped them over his ears as he waited for his tank to fill. Unlike her, he often complained about the cold. Peculiar, given he was born and raised here in the Rockies, and had spent his winters outside working the ski lifts.

Where Lindsay grew up, they were lucky if it snowed once or twice a year.

Gassed and ready to get going, Cody cranked both the ignition and the heater before he even pulled the Jeep's door closed. "Swear to God I'm moving to California before next season."

Lindsay said nothing. She'd tried California. Southern, Northern and in-between without finding much of anything that made her want to go back.

Cody turned left out of Ray's Service Station. The wrong direction.

"I thought we were going to the movies?"

He shook his head. "Want to show you something first."

"What?"

Cody shook his head again.

A few minutes later he turned off the pavement and into the National Forest. They'd come out to this area often back in the summer, to hike or mountain bike, but this time of year snow covered the ground most places. The twin beams of his headlights provided the only light for as far as the eye could see.

"Unless we turn around we won't make it over to Driggs in time to catch the movie."

He mumbled something but kept driving down the dark gravel and increasingly snow-packed, road until he had to slow down after fishtailing around an icy, uphill bend in the road.

"Where are we going?"

"I want to show you something," he repeated before adding, "but I might have to stop and lock in my hubs. Snow's deeper up here than I counted on."

"Just tell me where we're going."

"No. It's a surprise." He leaned forward to stare intently where his headlights stabbed through the darkness. He'd slowed way down, but still the Jeep slipped its way along, losing traction in the ever-increasing powder.

"Cody, this is stupid. We're going to get stuck out here." She gripped the sissy bar, dividing her attention between his tense face and the narrow, dark road. "And I'm not dressed to dig or push."

He grinned, but only for a second. "I've never been stuck in my life, but at least we'd have a good story to tell."

Cody was a horrible storyteller. He left out vital facts, rambled on getting off track often as not, and generally finished with broad assumptions based on the belief the rest of the world thought exactly as he did. Finding the point, or even the punchline, in his stories was like hunting a pine cone after a blizzard. Sure it was buried there somewhere, but never was it worth the effort it took to dig the thing up.

Just the fact he thought getting stuck in the snow—on a pitch black night—in the middle of nowhere, was anything but an exhibit of stupidity proved the point.

She could hear the old men now. Gathered at the counter of the Talon Cafe in the morning while she refilled their coffee mugs. *Yeah Joe, I reckon down there in Tulsa there ain't no snow to get stuck in.* She wasn't from Tulsa, but Lindsay was perfectly happy to let them be wrong on that front. *But up here in God's country, He chooses to weed out the tourists and tree-huggers by making life a bit more challenging.*

Joe, or Ray, or Stuart ... whoever happened to be within earshot would chime in, *Yep, ain't everybody cut out to be an Idahoan.*

They'd say it all with a smile and in a very poor imitation of her Oklahoma twang, but Lindsay wasn't dumb. The verdict on her was still out with most everybody except Cody and Janine. The Talon's regulars liked her well enough, but not enough to overlook the fact she was a foreigner in their world. Never mind the fact it was a Cody, a lifelong resident and true-blue Idahoan, driving them straight to Stupidville.

"Stop!"

Cody hit the brakes. The CJ-7 angled sharp right. They slid a solid twenty yards, but stopped three feet shy of a massive pine.

"What the hell?" He looked at her like she'd lost her mind.

In a way she had, but Lindsay couldn't go along with this journey not one more second.

"I'm freaked out, confused, and just a little pissed off you brought me out here this time of night when I thought we were going to the movie."

Cody was back to grinning, but she wasn't through. "It's not funny. When we get stuck. Not if, but when. Because if you keep barreling blind down this stupid, dark-ass road we certainly will get stuck. It won't be you forced to listen to every old man in town say, 'Damn Janine, these eggs are slimier this morning than a Targhee road come November.' They won't even mention your damn name. It will be mine, the tree-hugging, vegan, Southern girl that hears all about it."

He laughed. "Ahh hell, Linds, everybody is over that tree hugging, vegan stuff. We all figured out quick enough you weren't like that idiot you came here. He—"

Jabbing her finger at Cody she cut him off. "And if they do mention your name it will be Ray Everham saying something like, 'You and Cody shoulda gotta room at the Kozy-Inn. Hell, I'll set you up a cot in the g'rage of the Fill'n Station if you need a place that bad. Got a barrel of lube there and everything.'" *Even though she was trying to be funny, Lindsay still didn't like the fact Cody just kept grinning that stupid smile of his that displayed the small chip in his right front tooth. It made him look even younger than the twenty-five he'd just turned last week. Still four years and a few months younger than she.*

"Quit staring at me, and turn this damn thing around."

He shook his head. "Can't. You're too gorgeous for me to even look away."

She rolled her eyes.

"I like when you get all stoked up and your cheeks turn red."

"It's too dark in here for you to see my cheeks."

"It's not that dark."

He was right. What with his radio display, and the Jeep's headlights reflecting off the pine's large trunk, and the snow all around it wasn't near as dark inside the Jeep as it was down the stretch of road and surrounding forest. Still his flattery wasn't going to lead her where she didn't want to go.

"Wipe that look off your face, because if you think for a second I'm going to give Ray Everham's innuendos credence out here in the middle of this frozen damn forest, you're even crazier than he is."

Cody shrugged and dropped his voice a few octaves to say, "I'm here. You're here. There's not another soul around for miles."

"Turn the Jeep around."

"Your loss," he grinned and shifted in reverse. But the grin faded when the back wheel spun without grabbing hold. He tried a few more times. The CJ-7 rocked but didn't move.

He put his hands up at her pained expression. "Relax. I just have to lock in the hubs. We'll be out of here in minute." A wave of frigid air rushed in when he stepped out into the dark roadway.

Folding her arms across her chest, Lindsay stared beyond the pine tree right in front of her, out into the forest. Snow crystals glimmered under the headlights giving the scene the look of a fancy Christmas card.

Cody crossed in front of the Jeep, blocking the light for a second, thereby spoiling her respite from reality. If they got stuck out here all night, he dang sure wouldn't be singing "Winter Wonderland."

He crouched down by the front wheel for a minute before coming around to her side and opening her door. "Take the wheel for a second. I just wanna give a little push to make sure we get out." He stood back to let her get out of the Jeep. Using his teeth he pulled the glove off of his right hand as he stepped into the glow of the headlights.

Only in that half-a-heartbeat it took for him to drop to one knee, did Lindsay realize getting stuck in the snow was the least of her problems tonight.

Past experience should have made it easier for her to react. But no, she stood there—helpless, hopeless, heartless—and silently watched Cody pull that small velvet box from his pocket.

www.ingramcontent.com/pod-product-compliance
Lightning Source LLC
Chambersburg PA
CBHW020359080526
44584CB00014B/1090